Praise for *Platform Strategy*

'Ojanperä and Vuori's *Platform Strategy* is a unique book. It combines Ojanperä's hands-on experience of a senior executive grappling with the opportunities and threats of platform dynamics and Vuori's path-breaking work on the impact of affect and emotions on senior team action. As a result, *Platform Strategy* is an amazingly helpful book linking platforms and AI to an incumbent firm's shift in strategy and, in turn, organizational transformation. The uniqueness of this book is that it provides research-based and experience-based insights to help senior executives both think and feel their way through platform strategies. This book belongs on leaders' desks as well as academics' desks.' MICHAEL TUSHMAN, PROFESSOR, HARVARD BUSINESS SCHOOL AND AUTHOR OF *LEAD AND DISRUPT*, *WINNING THROUGH INNOVATION* AND *NAVIGATING CHANGE: HOW CEOS, TOP TEAMS, AND BOARDS STEER TRANSFORMATION*

'Creating a platform business and adopting AI are fundamental challenges for many organizations today. Ojanperä and Vuori build on their senior executive experience and top-tier research to provide a step-by-step guide for transforming your business. You learn how to manage both the hard business challenges and the softer human forces that determine whether you will succeed or fail.' LAURA HUANG, PROFESSOR, HARVARD BUSINESS SCHOOL AND AUTHOR OF *EDGE: TURNING ADVERSITY INTO ADVANTAGE*

'This book provides a comprehensive and cutting edge set of insights on how to succeed in deploying value-creating platforms, relying on state-of-the-art technologies such as AI and machine learning. It provides many practical step-by-step frameworks for executives to plan their implementation of platform-based offerings. One of the book's more distinctive values is that it combines both hard and soft considerations. The authors provide many useful insights related to hard aspects such as strategies, organizational structures and systems, and software technologies such as application programming interfaces (APIs). And they deftly combine these hard aspects with soft behavioural factors such as emotional energy, human creative thinking and responsible control over AI.' QUY HUY, PROFESSOR OF STRATEGY, INSEAD

'Platform business models together with AI create a new competitive advantage and superior value for customers. A clear and practical guide on how to build an Intelligent Platform with your team and external stakeholders.'
HENRIK EHRNROOTH, CEO, KONE

'This book provides hands-on guidance on how platform strategies, combined with the forces of data and AI, will create a competitive edge for companies regardless of industry. The authors' combination of research and in-depth experience provides leaders with the sense of urgency needed to be a winner in the future. Regardless of sector, companies will need the confidence to cooperate in smart and open eco-systems and thereby create greater outcomes together with partners. I especially appreciated the human-centric view on leadership and organizational impact to simplify governance and speed up the transformation for the benefits of customers, employees and society at large. Read it!' LUNDSTEDT MARTIN, CEO, VOLVO GROUP

'AI and platforms are common denominators for winning strategies in the future. Ojanperä and Vuori show how you can transform your business with lessons learned from the best companies in the world.' JOHN LINDFORS, MANAGING PARTNER, DST GLOBAL

'As C-Level executives or non-executive directors of technology companies, we all strive to stay current with the technologies that underpin the power and appeal of platforms and AI. The bigger challenge however is to distill this down to a set of practical priorities that are executable and scalable across distributed workforces. The authors explain in a practical way how to get started with building an intelligent platform to transform your business. But even more importantly, you will learn what you can do as a leader to drive change and help your team, colleagues, and external stakeholders succeed in an ever-increasing competitive world.' RICK SIMONSON, MANAGING PARTNER, SPECIE MESA LLC AND FORMER CFO, SABRE CORPORATION AND NOKIA

'This book brilliantly ties together the essential components needed for transforming your business using AI, platform thinking, and human creativity.' MÅRTEN MICKOS, CEO, HACKER ONE, FORMER CEO, MYSQL AND SENIOR VICE PRESIDENT, HP AND SUN MICROSYSTEM

'To build a successful platform and business takes actions in the right sequence to truly benefit and delight your customers and business partners.

The seven steps Ojanperä and Vuori outline provide a travel guide for this journey. Starting with energy, create value with focus, and ultimately multiply the benefits by creating the unexpected.' CHRISTIAN VON REVENTLOW, CTO OF MYREPUBLIC AND FORMER CHIEF PRODUCT OFFICER, TELSTRA AND DEUTSCHE TELEKOM

'AI and platforms drive digital transformation touching every industry segment. Opportunities to disrupt or be disrupted abound. In between the two extremes, components for sustainable competitive advantages are available for the fastest movers. *Platform Strategy* provides a straightforward seven-step program on how executives build and execute a strategy for the AI and platform era. Its unique approach builds on extensive research, numerous case studies, and practical guidance – a must-read book for leaders.' RISTO SIILASMAA, CHAIRMAN, F-SECURE CORPORATION AND FORMER CHAIRMAN, NOKIA

'A lot has changed. Everything from how we shop, socialize, and work and platforms are starting to work. Accelerated by the pandemic, those platforms thrive. One could even say it is the only way forward. *Platform Strategy* explains and showcases how digitalization and platforms are beginning to change how customers and companies engage. Platforms are creating new business opportunities for improving marketing, customer relationship management, and business strategy. Companies in many traditional industries are already taking steps to transcend industry boundaries and become intelligent platforms.

'As a tech founder myself, I enjoyed reading the wisdom and learned from the endless amounts of cases in *Platform Strategy*. Professor Timo O. Vuori and Dr Tero Ojanperä write in such a clear, inspirational, and action-oriented way that even the busiest founder and executive will find the book inspirational and helpful as a strategic tool.' SOULAIMA GOURANI, CEO AND CO-FOUNDER, HAPPIOH AND YOUNG GLOBAL LEADER, WORLD ECONOMIC FORUM

'Tero Ojanperä has been a thought leader in the AI space for many years and has always been a visionary leader and mentor. When we worked together at Nokia, he inspired me with his insights and emotional intelligence. He has since taken on many projects including launching Silo AI and becoming a researcher at several universities in Finland. Ojanperä and Vuori's book will inspire many senior executives to navigate organizational transformation effectively in the context of this new journey of platforms and AI. I couldn't be prouder of my former boss for this transformation piece of research.' LIZ SCHIMEL, FORMER HEAD OF BUSINESS, APPLE NEWS+, PRESIDENT, CONDÉ NAST INTERNATIONAL AND CHIEF DIGITAL OFFICER, MEREDITH CORPORATION

'Even the best companies need to renew themselves. The luxury industry is about connecting physical and digital with new business models to create customer value. One needs to move from product push to fulfilling customer needs and inspiring dreams and emotions throughout life. *Platform Strategy* provides a comprehensive but straightforward programme to start the digital transformation, including the necessary mindset change.' GEORGES KERN, CEO, BREITLING

Platform Strategy

*Transform your business with AI,
platforms and human intelligence*

Tero Ojanperä

Timo O. Vuori

KoganPage

First published in Great Britain and the United States in 2021 by Kogan Page Limited

2nd Floor, 45 Gee Street	122 W 27th St, 10th Floor	4737/23 Ansari Road
London	New York, NY 10001	Daryaganj
EC1V 3RS	USA	New Delhi 110002
United Kingdom		India
www.koganpage.com		

© Tero Ojanperä and Timo O. Vuori, 2021

The right of Tero Ojanperä and Timo O. Vuori to be identified as the authors of this work has been asserted by them in accordance with the Copyright, Designs and Patents Act 1988.

ISBNs
Hardback	978 1 3986 0268 7
Paperback	978 1 3986 0266 3
Ebook	978 1 3986 0267 0

British Library Cataloguing-in-Publication Data

A CIP record for this book is available from the British Library.

Library of Congress Cataloging-in-Publication Data

Names: Ojanperä, Tero, author. | Vuori, Timo O., author.
Title: Platform strategy : transform your business with ai, platforms and human intelligence / Tero Ojanperä, Timo O. Vuori.
Description: 1 Edition. | New York, NY : Kogan Page Inc, 2021. | Includes bibliographical references and index.
Identifiers: LCCN 2021028660 (print) | LCCN 2021028661 (ebook) | ISBN 9781398602663 (paperback) | ISBN 9781398602687 (hardback) | ISBN 9781398602670 (ebook)
Subjects: LCSH: Multi-sided platform businesses. | Strategic planning. | Artificial intelligence. | Creative ability in business. | Business enterprises–Environmental aspects.
Classification: LCC HD9999.M782 O53 2021 (print) | LCC HD9999.M782 (ebook) | DDC 338.7–dc23
LC record available at https://lccn.loc.gov/2021028660
LC ebook record available at https://lccn.loc.gov/2021028661

Typeset by Hong Kong FIVE Workshop, Hong Kong
Print production managed by Jellyfish
Printed and bound by CPI Group (UK) Ltd, Croydon CR0 4YY

Contents

List of Figures

About the authors

Dr Tero Ojanperä is a world-renowned technology business leader. The co-founder of Silo AI, one of Europe's largest private AI labs, he is an investor, venture capitalist and a valued board member in listed and non-listed companies. He was a member of the Nokia executive board as CTO and chief strategy officer. *Fast Company* crowned him the seventh most creative person in business and he is a Young Global Leader with the World Economic Forum. He lives in Helsinki, Finland.

Professor Timo O. Vuori is a strategy consultant and professor at Aalto University, a *Financial Times* top 40 business school. His ground-breaking research has focused on the human side of strategy making in technologically intensive organizations such as Nokia. Through consulting and executive education, Timo helps companies formulate and execute strategies, helping them transform into intelligent platforms. He lives in Helsinki, Finland.

Foreword

Platforms uniquely suited for a digital world

Digital platforms – or intelligent platforms as the authors call them in the book – are increasingly seen as path-breaking, perhaps even revolutionary new forms of organizing trading activities. The recognition of intelligent platforms having such potential is rather recent. When Apple launched its App Store in 2008, it was a low-key event compared to the launch of the iPhone. Few saw the potential of the App Store as a crucial complement to the iPhone. Walter Isaacson (2011), in his biography of Steve Jobs, reports that Jobs didn't want the App Store to be open to third-party developers, because he feared the loss of quality control. Pressure from the developer community eventually led him to take the risk.

Around the same time platform-native businesses began to emerge. Airbnb started in 2008 in San Francisco to meet the high demand of overnight rooms during large conferences. **Today Airbnb is a world-wide corporation with a market cap that exceeds Marriott's and Hilton's combined.** At the time of writing, there are thousands of platform businesses around the world. The US and China have been leading the way. Of the top ten most valuable companies on March 31 2021, eight are platform businesses: six from the US (Apple, Amazon, Facebook, Google, Microsoft, Tesla) and two from China (Ant Group, Tencent). Their aggregate market capitalization was US $10.48 trillion. Note that I count Tesla as a platform on wheels, which it is.

If one looks at the 100 most valuable unicorns in April 2021, close to 70 per cent of them are platform businesses and the platform momentum has increased since. Platform businesses continue to spread, threatening traditional businesses in many industries, directly and indirectly.

Much of the initial activity has been consumer oriented (B2C), but business-to-business (B2B) is expected to be the next big wave. All sectors will be affected, though there are obviously differences in the way businesses will respond. The boundaries between sectors will become blurred as mergers will increasingly be driven by expanding ecosystems where access to data often plays a bigger role than traditional connections. No business can feel indifferent about the on-coming reorganization. Every business should acquire an understanding of how platforms work and why they have been so successful in growing their business and achieving such high valuations.

Scalability and network effects

What are the drivers behind platform economics? Why have they taken over the top spots in market cap in such a short time?

Platforms create value by connecting buyers and sellers. That's what marketplaces have been doing for centuries as well as, in more recent times, shopping centres and stock markets, for instance. The scale of these platforms is limited by physical distance and other transaction costs. Intermediaries have bridged valuable gaps, but often at substantial cost.

Digital platforms can connect buyers and sellers at a much lower cost than traditional platforms or intermediaries. The business opportunities lie in eliminating frictions and eliminating intermediaries. The enablers are a confluence of digital technologies that complement each other.

Cloud computing, artificial intelligence, machine learning, blockchain and sensor technologies all contribute to safer and cheaper forms of transacting. The low cost of collecting, storing, processing and distributing digital information over the internet or 'in the cloud' have made digital platforms highly scalable. It is the scalability, especially in the B2C market, that has seen the market values of the most successful companies skyrocket. Another key driver is the network effects inherent to digital platforms. The more customers on a platform, the more valuable the platform is for new customers. Having reached a critical mass, a platform will keep growing at an increasing rate, often shutting out potential competitors. And the more users a platform has, the more data it generates.

Data is valuable for several reasons. It trains AI to become smarter, improving the accuracy of the prediction models. And it provides information that can be used to suggest individualized products and services or better buyer–seller matches. Data-based lending has given large populations in China, India and other parts of Asia access to credit. Information has become the new collateral, especially in poor regions where people have no registered wealth. Digital monitoring has also dramatically lowered the rate of fraud. This is another example of how digital technologies have reduced information costs and eliminated intermediaries.

Data is also driving the growth of ecosystems. Mergers across traditional lines of business are becoming increasingly common. The value of logistics firms has increased, because of the desirability of the data they possess rather than their transportation services. Understanding the increasing role of data and platforms is critical for foreseeing opportunities and risks in one's own markets.

The inverted firm

Platform Strategy focuses on how established businesses can embrace digital platforms and take advantage of the opportunities they present. The book offers lessons from a wealth of illustrative examples supported by the authors' extensive personal experiences and scholarly analyses. Everything written aims at helping executives and their companies find ways to adapt, stay relevant and grow with the help of platforms.

To become a platform business will require a big change in mindset – a new way of thinking strategically. Value is no longer captured by fostering long-term competitive advantages that rely on ownership of valuable assets and proprietary methods of production. Open interfaces give partners and customers access to company information and resources driving innovation and more value for the platform. This is done through APIs – Application Programming Interfaces – which provide algorithms for accessing data and tools to build third-party programs on top of the platform. The authors call the APIs 'algorithmic handshakes'. The APIs are gatekeepers that replace traditional intermediaries. Once written, the marginal cost of using APIs is minimal, because there is no human involvement.

When Amazon opened up its trading platform to third-party vendors in 2006 its sales exploded; today, third-party sales exceed Amazon's own. A few years later, Amazon did the same with its massively profitable cloud service, which today has 30 per cent of the share of the market (Srgresearch, 2021).

The payoffs from giving outsiders open access to platforms are many. Partners, old and new, will feel empowered and incentivized to come up with new opportunities and solutions. Amazon takes a share of the revenue, just like Apple does with the AppStore. Software-as-a-Service (SaaS) is a rapidly growing business model with great economic benefits. There will be less idle capacity and no need to distribute individual programs to customers. Platform owners get a steady income stream with lower investments in assets (though running cloud computers is expensive). And they get a share of the proceeds from an innovation system that they could never replicate within the company – again, without direct investments.

It takes courage and skill to run open platforms. The main strategic levers are still in the hands of the platform owner, who designs (or selects predesigned) APIs to be used on the platform. Still, there is not the same control over what kind of applications are built through the interface. Another constraint comes from the need to consider the effects changes to APIs have on network partners.

It is generally understood that ownership of assets gives firms the ability to coordinate activities more effectively. Markets transactions provide strong incentives, but ones that are biased towards own benefits. Cooperation is enhanced by bringing more assets under the same roof. Digital platforms offer a third option when evaluating the trade-off between cooperation and initiative, which lies somewhere between make and buy. Designing the playing field through APIs and orchestrating the game of cooperation are one of the challenges with a platform strategy.

A future without boundaries?

Platforms blur the boundaries of corporations as well as their lines of business. In 2002, Jeff Bezos issued his famous 'API mandate'; quoting from the book it began by stating that 'all teams will henceforth expose their data and functionality through service interfaces' (Kramer 2011). This made the internal workings of Amazon hugely more transparent. It required courage to open up the company to outsiders in such a revealing manner and showed Bezos' ability to foresee and control the future path of the platform business. The mandate was especially valuable for Amazon's cloud computing division AWS, which contributed around 60 per cent of Amazon's operating income in 2021. It integrated Amazon's internal and external interfaces, eliminating boundaries.

Haier, the world's largest white-ware company, has used a business model with even lesser distinction between inside and outside. Teams are formed as orders arrive, each bidding for the right to fulfill the order. Outsiders are free to come and bid as well. Outsiders can even lead teams consisting of Haier employees. Though Haier is a staple in business school curricula, the model has not spread (unlike Amazon's opening). Haier does have European and American units in which parts of the system are in place, but norms and legal rules have prevented full-scale adoption.

With these futuristic remarks, I'm suggesting that we are only seeing the beginnings of new, radically different, more open business models and forms of organization. Digital technologies have not eliminated the basic incentive and coordination problems that have defined boundaries in the past, but the trade-offs have changed in favour of more openness it appears.

Platform Strategy provides detailed, insightful advice for business executives on how to transform a company into an intelligent platform. The book combines deep business experience with concrete cases and cutting-edge, top quality academic research. It makes a convincing case for the value of platforms, underlining the importance of having a focused strategy that pays attention not just to technological solutions and analytical calculations, but equally to the human side of transitions. I'm confident that reading this book will mark the beginning of a transformational journey for many organizations.

Bengt Holmström
Nobel Laureate in Economic Sciences, 2016

References

Isaacson, W (2011) *Steve Jobs: The Exclusive Biography*, Simon & Schuster.

Kramer, S D (2011) The Biggest Thing Amazon Got Right: The Platform, *GigaOm*, https://gigaom.com/2011/10/12/419-the-biggest-thing-amazon-got-right-the-platform/ (archived at https://perma.cc/KAX6-KFER)

SrgResearch (2021) Amazon and Microsoft Maintain their Grip on the Market but Others are also Growing Rapidly, https://www.srgresearch.com/articles/amazon-and-microsoft-maintain-their-grip-market-others-are-also-growing-rapidly (archived at https://perma.cc/F96X-B2SK)

Preface

We wrote this book to help leaders lead and act on the disruption caused by platforms and artificial intelligence (AI).

There were many descriptive books on the platform economy and artificial intelligence. However, they did not provide clear enough guidance on transforming your current business into an intelligent platform or creating one from scratch. A straightforward recipe of how to get started and how to lead transformation was missing. That's what we wanted to address with the *Platform Strategy* book.

Our experiences and research had taught us that you cannot transform your business into an intelligent platform by changing it overnight. If you are too eager to copy everything that the successful ones do today, you will push too much too fast. Your platform strategy will fail to pace your actions effectively.

Tero's Nokia career was deeply embedded with platforms. Nokia's rise and fall is a story of platforms. After leaving Nokia in 2011, Tero focused on startup and investments, which helped him understand how businesses emerge. He also serves as a member of board of directors of listed and non-listed companies and has seen how boards struggle to address disruptive business models. In 2017, he co-founded Silo AI, an AI company that helps its clients transform business with AI.

Timo's research focuses on the human side of strategy making and innovation processes. He has conducted extensive case studies on Nokia and other major companies facing the digital and platform revolution since 2006. Through his work, he has learned how and why companies fail to transform and lead the change. He has also learned what successful companies do differently. He has refined these lessons in practice through executive education and strategy consulting since 2015. He has trained dozens of CEOs and helped several large companies develop new strategies and implement them.

Our paths collided in 2013 when on his research, Timo interviewed Nokia's former CEO Olli-Pekka Kallasvuo, who advised him to also talk to Tero. That interview seeded our collaboration. We met again in 2016, after the doctoral defense of Timo Ritakallio, the Group Executive Chairman of Finland's largest financial group, the OP Group and Timo's student. As we spoke, we realized the need to develop a better understanding of how to lead platform companies. That discussion kick-started our collaboration.

Platform Strategy brings together years of research, practical experiences and human insights on disruptive business models driven by AI and platforms. We hope *Platform Strategy* will help you as a business leader take the first step or accelerate your company transformation with AI, platforms and human intelligence.

Acknowledgements

Many people contributed to make this book happen. It's hard to remember all the valuable interactions we have had during the journey and probably we have forgotten some.

But in no specific order, thank you Timo Lappi, Wisa Majamaa, Mikko Kosonen, Yves Doz, Quy Huy, Olli-Pekka Kallasvuo, Pekka Koponen, Kari Pulli, Jaakko Soini, Teppo Paavola, Mark Borden, Johannes Koponen, Bengt Holmström, Matti Alahuhta, Henrik Ehrnrooth, Risto Siilasmaa, Timo Ritakallio, Atte Lahtiranta, Marco Argenti, Pekka Mattila, Elisabeth Pesola, Minna Wickholm, Raija Kuokkanen, Markku Mäkeläinen, André Noël Chaker, Liz Schimel, Mårten Mickos, Dave Stewart, Daniel Ek, Rick Simonson, Alf Rehn, Christian von Reventlow, Christian Juup, Oskar von Wendt, Niko Eiden, Hans Peter Brondmo, Matias Järnefelt, Taneli Ruda, Timo Toikkanen, Janne Öhman, Jussi Palola, Senja Larsen, Jukka Salmikuukka, Visa Friström, Tuomas Syrjänen, G Bailey Stockdale, Ari Tulla, Markus Salolainen, Eetu Karppanen, Tomi Pyyhtiä, Jussi Mäkinen, Toni Kaario, Helene Auramo, Kizzy Thomson, Wisa Koivunen, Tiina Mäkelä, Vesa Tuomi, Liisa Välikangas, Sven Smit, Joerg Hellwig, Klara Svedberg, Mikael Fristedt Westre, Bo Ilsoe, Atte Honkasalo, Waltteri Masalin, Upal Basu, Risto Rajala, Henry Schildt, Robin Gustafsson, Jane Seppälä, Suvi-Tuuli Helin, Christian Mohn, Lari Laukia, Reetta Repo and Matti Vestman; Peter Sarlin, Juha Hulkko, Ville Hulkko, Pauliina Alanen, co-founders, employees and customers of Silo AI; participants of Prodeko Life-Long Learning programme in 2019 and other Aalto University faculty and students who have provided comments and feedback; Soulaima Gourani, Thomas Crampton and other friends in the YGL community; Nokia colleagues; Tomi Ere and other colleagues at August Associates; Géraldine Collard our editor.

And a warm thank you to our families and loved ones for your support.

Introduction

Intelligent platforms are winning

It was early 2010. Nokia was the market leader in mobile phones with a global market share of over 30 per cent. A meeting between Steve Jobs and Nokia's CEO Olli-Pekka Kallasvuo had just taken place. Olli-Pekka, then Tero's boss, was shocked. He was mulling the words of Jobs in his mind. Jobs had said, 'I should not tell this to my competitors. But you are not my competitor, so I can tell you.' Reacting to Olli-Pekka's confusion, he had continued, 'You [Nokia] are not a platform. There is only one platform company other than Apple, namely Microsoft' (Siilasmaa, 2018).

But Nokia's not being a platform wasn't down to a lack of trying. At the time, Tero was in charge of building Nokia's services platform, Ovi. It was a diverse portfolio of services: music, photo sharing, social networks, video and TV. Nokia had acquired almost all of them. And these services were supposed to work over three operating systems: S40 for basic phones, Symbian for smartphones and Linux-based Meego for high-end smart-phones. As we know now, Nokia didn't succeed with smartphones. Although it managed to create some iconic phones like the N95 in 2008, it never developed a platform and a significant ecosystem.

Nokia had forgotten what made it the number one player in the world of phones – focus. In the early 1990s, under Jorma Ollila's leadership, Nokia moved from a conglomerate to a focused company. It shed various business such as forest-related products, TVs, computers, chemicals, cables and car tyres. The only thing Nokia kept was the mobile communications business. The dream team Jorma led, including Olli-Pekka (then CFO), focused on the emerging mobile phone business. It built one of the most influential brands in the world. But, it didn't last the next wave of innovation in smart-phones and platforms.

You don't build a platform by bolting many acquisitions together. Platforms evolve over time, step by step. You make a platform by having focus. Do one thing exceptionally well and then expand. And design your business and technical architecture for the expansion. Apple did it with the iPhone in 2007, with only one model but with a platform that others could innovate on. Similar to Apple, Tesla launched only one model, the model S, in 2016. Both had an architecture designed to evolve as a platform. Thus, Apple created the apps phenomena. And Tesla popularized self-driving cars.

But Apple is no longer a smartphone platform company. Over the years, it has evolved. It has leveraged its capabilities into new verticals, such as health and wellness, services with Apple One and vehicles, with the upcoming Apple car. Similarly, Tesla has entered the energy business in addition to the car business. Winners of the platform economy such as Amazon, Alibaba, Facebook and Tesla are transcending industry boundaries in that they are going beyond their industry segments. They capitalize on broader ecosystems, such as health and energy, that strengthen their offering and expand their commercial opportunities. With this book, you can learn to do the same.

These companies have become what we call *intelligent platforms*. Intelligent platforms generate network effects, have a learning loop powered by artificial intelligence (AI) and leverage human intelligence for unexpected leaps expanding their offering.

Now, you might think that this is only possible for the big and mighty. However, the lessons from companies that have transformed into intelligent platforms contain crucial elements for companies of many sizes. These include large industry incumbents seeking to retain their dominance and grow via platforms, and digitally native start-ups seeking to challenge the status quo and radically transform their industries.

A new approach to strategy

Companies in various traditional industries are already taking steps to transcend industry boundaries and become intelligent platforms. Consider freight forwarder Flexport, a company that is simplifying the archaic global logistics business. It achieves this by providing smart logistics solutions and expanding to non-traditional services such as trade advisory and financing.

The world's second-largest elevator company KONE focused on customer needs by understanding urbanization. For example, it developed a super-light elevator rope, KONE UltraRope, enabling elevators to travel to heights up to 1,000 metres (KONE, 2019). It also created the world's first digitally connected elevator series. But to expand beyond selling elevators and escalators, it needed an ecosystem of partners. KONE spent years exploring how to work with partners. Eventually, its head of partnerships decided to launch a platform for smart buildings. He engaged with the rest of the organization to win them over. Now KONE is connecting partners in intelligent ways to provide ever-smoother people flows. These flows bring in elements, such as robot minibars, that traditionally had nothing to do with elevators. They started with focus, refined their offering, made improvements and only then did they expand in creative and intelligent ways.

The number of companies that have already realized the power of intelligent platforms is snowballing. One of them is Lanxess, a German US $11 billion chemical company whose CEO and chief digital officer launched a platform, Chemodis. It is a business-to-business (B2B) marketplace that connects supply and demand to disrupt the chemical industry. Another example is John Deere, an agricultural manufacturing company. Ten years ago, its leaders saw an opportunity to foster innovation by working with partners. It connected its tractors and other equipment to a central digital cloud and opened the platform for partners. Through these moves, they not only avoided slow death but placed themselves in the driver's seat, creating new industries and tremendous growth.

For intelligent platforms, the use of data and AI to continuously improve their offering is central. For more than a century, Thomson Reuters has been collecting massive amounts of proprietary data. Essential insight for its business leaders was that the question was not 'What can AI do?' but 'What problems can AI solve?' (Thomson Reuters, 2020). It focused on how to help legal professionals. For this, Thomson Reuters trained its legal service Westlaw Edge with proprietary data. With an AI-based learning loop, every customer query further improves the system. In this way, they are continually learning more, thus improving their service and engaging more customers. And more customers mean more data and further accelerated learning.

The traditional way of doing strategy suggests firms should focus on a specific industry, select an optimal position and develop capabilities that suit that position. Diversification to unrelated industries has been seen as a hubristic mistake; true leadership results from a vision that aligns firm actions toward a specific goal. Even those approaches that emphasize strategic agility tend to consider it from a narrow perspective. The thinking goes that firms should be agile within their current industry, rapidly developing their products and taking various kinds of competitive actions. Instead of opening up executives' thinking and leveraging the platform era's new possibilities, they amplify their myopic attention to the present industry and traditional ways of conducting business.

In contrast, we argue that a new way of doing strategy has emerged. The leading firms no longer define themselves in terms of traditional industry boundaries. Instead, they actively seek to transcend the boundaries and create synergistic value across industries. They can do this because platform business models and AI tools enable them to combine traditionally incompatible activities. But this ability is not based on technology alone – their leaders need the human qualities of creative insight to see the opportunities and courage to take action.

For example, Ant Financial, a spin-out from Alibaba, established a strong foundation in one vertical, financial services, with its Alipay payment platform (Ojanperä and Vuori, 2020). After that, it started to build a 'one-stop digital lifestyle platform' that connects 40 million service providers, including grocery-delivery companies, hotels and transportation companies (Alipay, 2020).

Although business leaders of established companies recognize new technologies' possibilities, they have difficulties applying them in their current business. As a result, they get paralysed and overwhelmed by industry news and demands of change from the board and employees. We help you avoid this trap. We tell you concretely what you need to do and in which order you need to do those things.

The elements of an industry-transcending platform strategy

To transcend industry boundaries, your firm needs to have three crucial elements in place and think of your strategy as a sequence of steps over time. The three factors are: 1) network effects via a platform approach, 2) AI-enabled learning loop and 3) the active use of human intelligence, insight and creativity. The chapters of this book describe the seven steps through which you can build the three crucial elements for your business, but first, let's look at each of these three factors in more detail.

Network effects via a platform approach

The first element consists of a platform approach that generates network effects. Platforms enable multiple other parties to create value by combining their efforts and facilitating interaction. The value of a platform grows as the number of users, interactions and platform use increases, thus creating a *network effect*.

Having only a single telephone in the world would be pointless. Having two phones would enable two people to communicate. Having thousands of phones allows millions of connections between people. It makes the phone far more valuable for each phone owner. This is a *direct network effect*. Another example of a direct network effect is Amazon marketplace customer reviews and recommendations. The more users, the more reviews and recommendations, and thus value to other Amazon users.

In indirect network effects, the value of one group of users grows as the number of users in the other group grows. For example, iPhone developers and customers create indirect network effects. The more there are of each, the more they benefit. The more developers, the larger the variety of apps available and, hence, the more value for the customer. And the more potential customers there are, the higher expected sales for an application developer, and the more revenue the platform can provide for them.

John Deere connects multiple agriculture parties, including machines, farmers, farm management systems and application developers. Each new party strengthens the indirect network effect. As a result, machines produce more data that application developers can use. More farm management systems connected to the platform increase its attractiveness to farmers. And the more applications there are, the better for farmers who use the platform to optimize their farming activity.

Due to their inherent nature, network effects generate long-lasting benefits. The platform gets better over time, making it even more attractive for new customers and other platform stakeholders to join. Furthermore, due to network effects, it becomes evermore difficult for people to leave the platform. They are unlikely to get matching benefits from less developed platforms.

In addition to benefitting from network effects, a platform model enables companies to assemble new capabilities rapidly. This is crucial when they are seeking to expand their offering or transcend industry boundaries. Instead of developing a new ability organically or through an acquisition, a platform model allows the company to offer third-party services to their customer via the platform.

An application programming interface (API) is a mechanism to connect new applications to the platform. From the customers' point of view, it looks like the platform has the capability, and hence they choose to buy it from the platform. Just like it feels that iPhone has all the great functionalities that third-party application developers provide. Or how John Deere, instead of just selling machines, also offers applications using data from them to increase farmers' productivity. Hence, a platform approach takes innovation to an entirely different level than what any company operating in a single industry can reach.

AI-enabled learning loop

Intelligent Platforms have an AI-powered learning loop that rapidly improves their value creation and efficiency in new domains. Once they have entered the industry, they 'run' faster than the incumbents or other entrants and quickly provide more value than others.

AI-enabled learning loops consist of cycles of action, data analysis and revision of actions. In each step, various data about the action and its outcomes are measured. Multiple actions and their outcomes are also compared to one another. In this way, you can determine which qualities of actions lead to better results. Hence, in the next round, you can add those qualities to all actions and perform better. Furthermore, you can intentionally experiment with various alternative measures and keep those that improve performance while ditching the others. As you repeat this cycle, again and again, your performance improves steadily, and you cumulate superior ability to perform the focal task.

While the learning loop is similar to natural human learning, there is one crucial difference: the speed and experience cumulation. A single human can reflect on their own actions and outcomes and, perhaps, on those of a few colleagues. This produces some learning. But an AI system can accurately record and systematically reflect on the actions and outcomes of thousands or millions of people, enabling a totally different magnitude of learning.

Furthermore, humans have difficulties in admitting their mistakes and accepting that their initial ideas were wrong. In contrast, AI has no such problems. Hence, AI not only learns more and faster, but it also learns more accurately. It is free from ego-defences and other psychological hindrances to learning.

Human intelligence, insight and creativity

Third, intelligent platforms leverage human intelligence, creativity and courage to make unexpected leaps expanding their offering scope. They are not bound by traditional industry or product-specific identities. Instead, they see synergistic opportunities across distant sectors and are not afraid to act on those opportunities. Effectively, they bring remote industries together by building a technology-enabled 'wormhole' between the industries that others could not even imagine.

Human insight and creativity are needed because AI, despite all of its virtues, still isn't very creative. Amazon would never have moved from selling books to selling other items and cloud services by using AI to optimize its book sales. Apple would never have moved from making computers to making iPods and iPhones by using AI to analyse which kinds of computers people like. Fundamentally, category-breaking strategic moves require human creativity. AI is good within boundaries, but to transcend industry boundaries, you need human insight.

To use human insight and creativity productively in your organization, you need to manage your organization's psychology. People's insights come from their brains, and various organizational factors influence their brains. You need to understand how your people think and feel and why they think and feel the way they do. Then you can change the factors that activate counter-productive behaviours and add factors that stimulate their intelligence, insight and creativity.

Seven steps for building an industry-transcending platform strategy

Creating a strategy to transcend your industry requires you to manage three interdependent dynamics: 1) creating network effects, 2) adopting AI and 3) developing human creativity and courage to leap to new domains. As fear can paralyse your firm from adopting the new technology and revising its business model, you need to start by turning fear into energy. However, this energy provides valuable results only if you make the right technology and business model choices. Again, those choices only enable you to continue the transformation if you find the courage and creativity to transcend industry boundaries.

Hence, you need an approach that helps you synchronize and synergize between AI, network effects and psychology over time to enable radical transformation. We provide such an approach in seven steps based on research and case studies on how platform economy winners have developed their business over time. The figure below outlines these steps.

FIGURE 0.1   Seven steps to become an intelligent platform

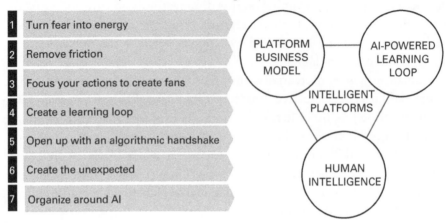

Tesla illustrates these steps well. As other auto manufacturers held back due to fear of new technology, Elon Musk *turned the fear of the unknown into energy* and a powerful force of change. With superchargers, Tesla *removed friction* from charging your electric vehicle. Tesla *started with a well-focused approach* of one luxury car for environmentally conscious customers to build momentum. Its autonomous driving was not perfect, but due to the *learning loop*, it develops faster than the competition.

Tesla has also started to open up its platform for third-party applications. This enables *algorithmic handshakes* via application programme interfaces (APIs) that allow computer programmes to communicate directly between them. And Tesla *creates the unexpected* by leveraging its battery, analytics and design capabilities by expanding into home energy storage systems. Boosting its effectiveness and reaching the full potential of platforms and AI, Tesla is increasingly *organizing its activities around AI*. It employs AI to replace formal hierarchy for managing and coordinating various operations.

Chapter 1 describes how you need to *turn fear into energy*. Becoming an intelligent platform changes your organization in radical ways. This triggers fear in many people – among your executive team, employees and potential partner firms. As a result, their worries can cause inertia and prevent your transformation. To turn these fears into energy, you need to make conscious structural and processual choices and apply several psychological techniques. Building on our practical experience and latest top-tier research (Vuori and Huy, 2016a, 2016b, 2018), we describe these choices and techniques in a practical way.

Chapter 2 shows how *removing friction* from your operations and simplifying things for your customers builds a strong foundation for your platform. Platform business models are effective because they combine multiple actors to work together. This is meaningful only if it happens without friction. Friction results from transaction cost. In this chapter, you learn how you can minimize the three fundamental transaction costs: search and effort costs, uncertainty and anxiety costs, and opportunism-related costs. Our chapter shows how to increase trust and controls in your platform in clever ways, such as rating systems, without overly complicating the platform use.

Chapter 3 tells you you need to *focus your actions to create fans*. Having identified businesses or processes from which to remove friction, you are ready to launch a spearhead that will engage more people and start expanding your platform. The initial, narrow focus on a spearhead allows you to do one thing exceptionally well – like iPhone and Tesla with one product only. This engages the customers and keeps them committed, contributing to the build-up of network effects. You learn how to identify a lucrative focus area and take initial actions.

Furthermore, once companies have found their focus, they refine their offering and build an engaged community. You learn various practices by which you can steadily and continuously improve your focus area. As a final element, you gain knowledge of how to build a community through multiple methods, such as by enabling communication between your platform stakeholders. The engaged community strengthens network effects and provides valuable insights for you for further improving your platform.

Chapter 4 helps you discover how an *AI-enabled learning loop* enables you to improve the focused offering and engagement extremely fast and effectively. An AI-enabled learning loop is a systematic approach for collecting and analysing data from your actions to improve those actions. The improvements can relate to cost-efficiency, product or service quality, customer engagement and various other desirable outcomes. To reach meaningful enhancements, you need to start with business goals. It is too easy to envision various AI applications and get lost in meaningless data and reports. But when you define business goals, your AI efforts directly improve your platform. You also learn how to produce relevant data to enable AI use and various practices to maximize continuous learning from the data. This chapter shows particularly compelling examples from Tesla, Uber and Orica (an explosive provider) on each aspect of building a learning loop.

Chapter 5 starts opening up the game – it discusses how you can use *an algorithmic handshake* to involve more actors in your platform. New actors can include new customers, third-party service providers and various types of suppliers. They are incredibly willing to join your platform. This is due to the excitement you have created by your focused offering, which you have radically improved via an AI-enabled learning loop. An algorithmic handshake enables companies to join your platform smoothly by allowing direct communication and contracting between computers without human involvement. Technically, it happens through application programming interfaces (APIs). You learn how to define business goals for API and how to develop APIs as a product. You will also master a lifecycle view to APIs, which is essential for your platform's long-term evolution.

Chapter 6 takes you to the creative side. So far, you have created a focused offering and improved it via an AI-enabled learning loop and third parties through algorithmic handshakes. Next, we will show you how to *create the unexpected*. You can take radical leaps from your prevailing industry. These are unforeseen moves because, from a traditional business perspective, such diversification makes no sense. However, platforms and AI enable you to effectively and synergistically combine activities in distant industries in value-adding ways. You learn three specific approaches for developing radical insights that become your unexpected moves. We have created these approaches by applying the latest research on strategic management and creativity in various companies. This allows us to describe practically and concretely how you can use these practices in your organization.

Chapter 7 shifts the focus from what new offering you should provide for the markets to how you can most effectively deliver what you have promised by *organizing around AI*. The central idea you will remember for the rest of your career is that you should replace formal hierarchy with AI-enabled coordination whenever possible. You will also learn how to work with AI. You will start by familiarizing yourself with AI and using AI as an additional adviser. Eventually, you will learn to trust the AI and let it autonomously analyse and implement the best decisions. We will also show you how to get rid of physical restrictions in development with digital twins.

These seven steps will change your mindset, and you will start to think differently about how to create value and expand your business.

CHAPTER ONE

Turn fear into energy

B ecoming an intelligent platform might seem like a technological challenge. Our research shows that it is also a psychological one, which is
steeped in irrational fear. Intelligent platforms challenge many of your business's underlying assumptions, including ways of working that organizations
have honed for years that may need to change.

For example, the smartphone business transformed into a platform business after the introduction of the iPhone. Instead of offering alternative
phone models with only pre-defined software applications, Apple enabled
customers to download third-party applications via the App Store. These
applications revolutionized how people used their phones.

Nokia was the industry's titan at the time, and its leaders had to rethink
the idea of a phone. The company had succeeded by producing dozens of
different models of phones. In contrast, the platform model would have
required it to reduce the number of models. Its operating system's quality
also required a quantum change to make it easier for third parties to develop
applications for Nokia phones. This was crucial as third-party application
developers drove the network effect. As a result, Nokia's board and top
management team experienced severe discomfort and fear (Vuori and Huy,
2016a). And as we know it now, Nokia was late to the smartphone game.

And yet, fear does not need to slow you down. Instead, you can use this
very fear to your advantage. Fear is among the strongest human emotions.

Once you channel its energy for growth and expansion, your organization becomes unstoppable.

Electric vehicles, the cloud and self-driving cars have created havoc in the automotive industry. New entrants such as Tesla, like Apple when it introduced the iPhone, play the platform game. Volkswagen wants to avoid Nokia's fate, and its CEO Herbert Diess has recognized the threat of being unseated: 'The era of the classic carmakers is over […] The big question is: Are we fast enough?' (Reuters, 2020). His challenge is to help executives, the organization and partners overcome the fear of change and move fast enough.

In this chapter, we describe tools to make this transition easier. These help you to start your transformation towards becoming an intelligent platform. There are three types of fear to overcome that affect three different stakeholder groups in your organization:

- Executives: paralysis and panic.
- Organization: rigidity and resistance.
- Partners: scepticism and distrust.

You can turn each type of fear into energy through the actions we present in this chapter.

Executive fear: paralysis and panic

Fear prevents organizations from successfully transforming into platform businesses and adopting AI. It often manifests in paralysis and panic which hold us back. Fears diminish our intelligence by narrowing our thinking and blocking creativity.

Some leaders get paralysed. As they have recognized the importance of platforms, sleepless nights follow. They imagine their demise as new platform companies steal their customers. However, they cannot visualize what they should do. Hence, following the age-old instinct, they hide.

They feel the threat cannot touch them as long as they remain hiding. Prey has a similar reaction to the entry of a predator. Cognitively, fear makes them narrow minded and risk averse. They avoid taking any bold stance or action, as it would make them more visible. Of course, the last thing prey wants to do is become visible if the threat is near.

And they do not want to pick a fight with the predator either. Instead, if they cannot hide from public attention, they will go into denial. That is, they will lie to themselves that the threat is not there, like a kid who covers their eyes in front of a TV when Pennywise the Clown is just about to strike one of his victims.

Tesla launched the Model S in 2016. Since then, it has already launched several alternative models. Disruption keeps speeding up. The rest of the industry, in response, was paralysed. Only in 2020 did Volkswagen announce cuts to fuel cells to invest more into electric vehicles (Reuters, 2020). Tesla has already moved on. The company is experimenting with new business models powered by its full self-driving software and its insurance and ride-sharing businesses. It has also entered new industries altogether with forays into home energy systems with Tesla Powerwall and Solar Roof.

In 2007, Nokia executives stated that Apple's iPhone would 'stimulate this market [and be] good for the industry' (Forbes, 2007). The statement illustrates the effects of fear. Nokia did not cover its eyes literally, but mentally. Cognitively, the Nokia team knew that the 'iPhone was an extension of Mac—a Mac computer with radio added. [Apple had] been building the applications and the OS for 35 or 40 years' (Vuori and Huy, 2016a). But still, their fear generated the illusion that Nokia would benefit from its entry. Nokia had started to design touchscreens and an app store already before 2005. However, fear and paralysis prevented fast enough progress.

Leaders often panic. They see that the threat is imminent and that they must do something. Unfortunately, their emphasis is more on the 'do' and less on defining the 'something'.

Their panic can take many forms. For example, some start reshuffling their organization. They name new leaders and change formal structures. They may also propose new processes and initiate a large number of consulting projects.

If the internal efforts are not sufficient to ease the panic, leaders may also take more extensive actions. Typical measures include massive investments in vague innovation projects, risky acquisitions and flashy but abstract presentations about radical shifts and the future.

In the 2010s, car companies panicked over three threats: self-driving cars, electric vehicles and ride sharing. Following the success of Uber, many decided to bet on ride sharing. BMW launched a ride-sharing service ReachNow in 2018. Daimler teamed up with Via to launch a ride-sharing shuttle service. In 2019, BMW and Daimler joined forces with a joint venture, FreeNow. However, these services failed to reach scale. In autumn 2020, Uber considered buying FreeNow (Freitag, 2020).

All of these moves seem to make sense on the surface. However, they failed to recognize that they would need to create a compelling, focused product and service that gets to scale to succeed. We will discuss how focus makes fans and enables scaling in Chapter 3. Even more importantly, the automotive disruption was a battle of platforms. Doubling down on electric vehicles won't help unless one builds a software platform to go with it.

Facing a threat from Facebook, Google and Amazon, the communication giant Verizon built a platform business. It acquired AOL and Yahoo and merged them under the name Oath. It admitted defeat in 2019 and made a US $5.6 billion write-off.

In 2012, Microsoft announced a new strategy. It wanted to create seamless experiences across hardware, software and services. Its strategy was similar to Apple, a company it feared so much. The US $7 billion acquisition of the Nokia device business was Steve Ballmer's panic move. Satya Nadella undid it. A US $7 billion write-off and layoffs of 7,800 employees followed. But, Nadella also turned fear into energy. He focused the company on cloud computing. Microsoft was a player again.

Finland's largest commercial bank is the OP Group. Digitalization and platforms have undermined traditional banks' position. The CEO predicted in 2017 that hundreds of branches would close down, and thousands of people would lose jobs (YLE, 2017). This prediction was correct. But then the company panicked. The company ventured into a car-sharing business. It also expanded into housing services and various other domains. Later, one by one, the bank closed down the ventures. The company focused back on its core banking service, facing the fear with an active approach to digitalization.

But there is no need to panic. Initial paralysis does not need to be fatal as disruptions usually take time. The typical cycle is 10 years. But you need to recognize the signs and start to move early enough with a long-term view.

Why do executives fear platforms and AI?

Companies always fear new things that can destroy them. Platforms and AI are no exception. Any radical change in the business landscape and new competition are enough to drive many incumbents into oblivion. That's enough reason for being afraid.

And yet, platforms and AI also have characteristics that generate more fear than other types of changes. It is not just a new competitor who does things a bit better. Or new legislation that favours somewhat different companies. No, platforms and AI change the fundamental logic of business, organizations and industries. They make much of what you have learned invalid. And that's scary on a different level.

Loss of control

Platforms mean that you have partners, not subordinates. Thus, you have no hierarchical power over them, nor can you have a real handle over their plans and performance. Hence, you are likely to feel less in control, and this loss of control generates fear.

Even Steve Jobs feared depending on partners. Initially, he didn't want third-party apps for the iPhone. But, after a backlash from developers, he changed his mind. Twelve years later, App Store revenue is about US $54 billion (Statista, 2020).

A radical change in the business model

When you become an intelligent platform, you also need to challenge many traditional ideas about how your business works. The platform business model radically differs from the traditional one.

For example, adopting a platform approach might result in your company's revenue declining significantly. Still, your profits, in absolute terms, might get multiplied because royalties often form the basis for platform business models. However, such a decline in revenue can make stakeholders perceive that the new model makes the company smaller. Consequently, people's anger and fear prevent them from even considering becoming an intelligent platform.

Reduced room for personal judgement

The increased adoption of digital technology increases the amount of data for decision-making. As a consequence, companies can automate many decisions that previously required executive judgement. This development can create a personal threat for executives because their expertise and judgement define their identity. Many leaders define themselves as superior decision-makers. They have their '35 years of experience' that makes them valuable. Suppose an AI algorithm promises to make excellent decisions.

In that case, these leaders may feel their distinctive feature, which is their decision-making skill, has become irrelevant.

For example, AI can predict when parts fail in a factory with astonishing accuracy. However, an experienced factory manager might not trust the prediction. After all, the manager has tens of years of experience; why would the machine know better? Hence, they might actively campaign against the use of AI. They might even create situations in which the AI algorithm fails, such as untypical conditions that make algorithms based on prior data less accurate.

Four steps to turn executive fear into energy

How do you as an executive fight emotion from loss of control, a radical change in the business model and reduced room for personal judgement? And more importantly, how do you get your team to do the same? We explain the four steps needed to succeed.

Four steps to turn executive fear into energy

1 Create psychological safety and collective mindfulness

2 Create and evaluate options

3 Identify the smallest action with the highest impact for each option

4 Approach potential partners early on

---

1. Create psychological safety and collective mindfulness

Behind all fears is the fundamental fear of not surviving something. Often, executives do not recognize the fear in themselves but project it to the strategic situation or other people. The sense of personal threat amplifies their anxiety about the company situation and complicates discussions about difficult strategic topics.

A toxic discussion culture amplifies personal fear. For example, people make nasty remarks about others' comments and verbally abuse people who share difficult news or critical viewpoints. Hence, you first need to fix the discussion culture.

Executive infighting and backstabbing were hallmarks of Microsoft's toxic culture (Eichenwald, 2012). When becoming CEO in 2014, Satya Nadella asked his executive team members to read *Nonviolent Communication* (Rosenberg, 2003). The book outlines four principles for effective communication:

- Observe what happened. Avoid any judgement or criticism.
- State how you feel when you observe the situation.
- Articulate what need of yours is not satisfied.
- Request a concrete action to meet that need.

Seldom has one book resulted in such a fundamental change. Of course, there was much more work needed. However, Nadella's application of the book was the cornerstone for the new Microsoft.

An increasing number of management teams have started using explicit discussion rules for increasing psychological safety. For example, Risto Siilasmaa, Nokia's chairman of 2012–20, introduced seven Golden Rules for board discussions (Siilasmaa, 2015). These rules include, for example:

- Assume the best of intentions in the actions of others. Operate openly, honestly and directly and expect others to do the same.
- Be prepared for a passionate debate, but do it in an informed and respectful way. Then affirmatively support the decisions that arise, even if you did not win the argument.
- Firmly and respectfully challenge the management while keeping in mind that the board is successful only when the CEO and management team are successful.

He also reinforced the rules. When a board member or top manager deviated from them, he would speak with the person offline. Then the deviant executive would apologize in the next meeting (Vuori and Huy, 2021).

Netflix preaches a culture of candor. The company encourages direct feedback from everybody to anybody, including directly to the CEO. But the way Netflix employees give feedback is critical. It starts with a rule: always assume the best intentions of the giver. And feedback must be actionable (Hastings and Mayer, 2020).

In addition to the threat of hostile communication, the loss of control is a fundamental force that reduces psychological safety when companies move toward platforms. Therefore, it is essential to increase the sense of control during the strategy-making process. You can do this by specifying precise process steps for your strategizing. You may not control what happens in the environment, nor do you know beforehand what your company should choose. But you can influence how you approach the task. Thus, you gain confidence and turn your fear into energy. You no longer run in circles but progress forward.

Amid the uncertainty, part of the fear is not knowing what you should do while you feel the urgency to do something. A simple solution, though temporary, is to choose to do nothing. To ease your fear, you and your executive team could decide to take one to two months to understand what is happening in the external reality. And you should do this without any attempts to find solutions.

This approach puts you in a state of mindfulness, where you open up perception and accept things as they are. You simply seek to understand. You go from being a first-person subject to a third-person observer. You start seeing the bigger picture, patterns of actions and causal forces. You get satisfaction from the higher-order understanding.

Practically, you can:

- summarize external trends;
- interview company stakeholders and even competitors;
- assess internal and external situations;
- assess changing consumer behaviour.

2. Create and evaluate options

Extensive psychological research shows our brain generates a fear reaction when two conditions occur. First, the external situation is somehow threatening our well-being or success. And second, we do not know what we can do about the situation. A threatening situation is not scary if we know we can deal with it. For example, if you face a mugger alone in a dark alley, you will likely feel fear because you don't know if you can avoid the beating. However, if you have bodyguards with you, you feel much less worried because you know they will protect you.

Strategic options are like bodyguards – they give you a way to deal with a threatening situation.

Currently, new competition enabled by platforms threatens your business. However, if you generate a potential strategic option, your chances of successfully fighting the new competitor increase. If you develop several alternatives, your chances increase even more. Hence, options reduce your fear.

You should seek to create options, even in situations where you think that you have no options. Fear causes narrowing down your thinking, which is why you think you have no options. So, force yourself to create an alternative, even a bad one. As a result, you become less anxious. And you can think a bit more broadly, leveraging your human intelligence. Again, this reduces your fear and lets you create more and better options than ever.

Once you have created several options, you should also start critically evaluating them. You should identify what the critical assumptions behind each option are.

For example, an option of going into a particular business model might assume specific technological breakthroughs. Or widespread use of AI might require a revamp of the company's data infrastructure. Once you have recognized such assumptions, you can also assess their validity. Through this process, you understand which options are the likeliest to succeed. Such scrutiny will increase your confidence in the ultimate choice. You know for sure that it is the best option out of all the options you could have imagined.

3. Identify the smallest action with the highest impact for each option

No matter which option you choose, you will need to take several actions to create an intelligent platform. You need to invest in technological development in multiple modules, reach several markets, recruit new talent, introduce new products and so on. It can feel overwhelming and bring back the paralysing fear, even if you already started to feel energized.

Hence, it's essential to take small actions that generate a significant impact. These are actions that are relatively low cost and low risk, and, as such, do not overly stimulate fear. Simultaneously, they should have a visible impact so that they excite people and generate more energy. Furthermore, they should build a steppingstone for your next actions.

Hence, as a part of the systematic process of turning executive fear into energy, you need to build a path from the present situation to the target state. For full strategizing, you can use the methods we introduce in Chapter 6, 'Create the unexpected', and the backtracking method we introduce in Chapter 3. To turn fear into energy, you need to remember the essential elements: imagine all the significant steps required for the option to be realized; reflect how you can take the steps in different sequences; identify which sequence starts with the smallest effort and highest impact.

For example, Tetrapak provides solutions and services for the food and beverage industry. It created a vision towards manufacturing-as-a-service. For this, it needed better data from factories. In 2019, as the first step towards the vision, it launched a B2B marketplace for spare parts – more on that in Chapter 3, 'Focus your actions to create fans'.

In addition to reducing fear related to taking the first step, this approach creates a sense of continuity. Continuity is good because it minimizes the identity threat imposed by the new platform direction.

Furthermore, when you recognize potential pivoting points and paths in advance, fear related to any option is minimized. You can also identify how you might pivot after each step to the other tracks that you have imagined.

4. Approach potential partners early on

Compared to traditional business models, a core uncertainty in platform business models is the engagement of partners. Network effects generate value in platforms but, without partners, their value is zero. Furthermore, you cannot know beforehand if the partners you do get will generate value.

To reduce these uncertainties and turn your associated fear into energy, you should approach potential partners early on. When you interact with other companies, you get a sense of whether they will join your platform or not. And you get a sense of whether they will be able to contribute or not.

You do not need to start with formal negotiations. Informal lunches and brainstorming sessions help you understand if you are on the same page and if they might be interested. Incrementally, you can reveal and propose more if you sense that they are sincere and curious.

As you learn which partners are enthusiastic and able to contribute, your fear of not finding a proper partner diminishes. You free up energy for further envisioning the platform and taking action.

Chapter 5, 'Open up with an algorithmic handshake', will discuss how the global manufacturer of elevators, KONE, created a partner programme to succeed with its Application Programming Interfaces (APIs). As APIs enable the computers of KONE and its partners to interact without human involvement, they revolutionize people-flow solutions for buildings with KONE elevators.

Organizational fear: rigidity and resistance

While executives' fear causes failed decisions, fears spreading in the organization cause rigidity and resistance. Middle managers and employees who fear the novel technologies and new business models stifle transformation and growth with non-conscious rigidity and active resistance.

In the early 2000s, leading American newspapers saw the threat imposed by online media. Many of their executives overcame their fear and invested substantially in new media operations. They hired technological expertise and new staff and launched websites. Unfortunately, as shown by research conducted at Harvard University (Gilbert, 2005), they did not leverage the latest technology's possibilities but instead simply replicated the printed newspaper on the web. It was almost like the new media department took a printed copy of the morning's paper, scanned it and uploaded it onto the website.

The behaviour of these newspapers illustrates fear-based rigidity in the organization. Even though the newspapers' staff wanted to adapt, their fear made them stick to their traditional thinking. They took the newspaper industry's norms for granted and did not create novel services. When people are afraid, they find recourse from tradition. And as fear narrows down cognitive processes, it causes them to simply end up doing what they have always been doing. This can happen even when companies initiate change programmes and the staff is motivated.

Many organizations are currently trying to adopt platform business models in the same way as the rigid newspaper companies of the early 2000s. They want to create a multi-sided platform with many innovative partners. Still, they also want to have hierarchical control over the partners and strict, linear processes. They want to create learning loops and leverage big data with multiple partners but refuse to share their data with them.

In 2020, Disney launched its streaming service Disney+, 12 years later than Netflix. Other traditional media companies are now following the suit. But why did it take so long? Because they are victims of their success, and fear has paralysed them. It is hard to move to a new model when they optimized the business for the old model. Movies launch first in theatres, later in other channels. Changing consumer habits, however, challenged this model.

Microsoft embraced the platform business model early on, and Windows was extremely successful. However, when the industry moved on to mobile and cloud, Microsoft was still optimizing everything around Windows, neglecting Android and iOS platforms.

Fear also generates active resistance that slows down your path towards becoming an intelligent platform. Employees fight because they feel they are under threat. Even the smartest people can develop this reaction, as shown by a Harvard University study on NASA (Lifshitz-Assaf, 2018).

CASE STUDY   Fear and resistance at NASA

NASA chose to adopt open innovation practices in 2009 to increase its productivity and problem-solving ability. They used open innovation practices to open up NASA to external people for problem-solving purposes. Essentially turning NASA into a platform that matched internally recognized problems with external problem-solvers.

However, traditionally, NASA's internal staff had worked on the technological problems related to space missions exclusively. The engineers prided themselves on being world-leading problem solvers. For them, opening up NASA to outside expertise was a threat and an insult. For example, the innovation lead described:

> When you asked [whether you have an R&D problem to share], they'd [engineers] say, 'You want me to tell you what I can't solve?' It was very much like they would be exposing some kind of incompetency if staff told us what they can't do [...] They thought, 'You are asking others [on open innovation platforms] to solve it for us.' You can see people physically uncomfortable with it in their body language. (Lifshitz-Assaf, 2018: 757)

Even though NASA would improve its problem-solving ability by turning it into a platform, many of its most valuable members feared and resisted this move. Consequently, they refused to share problems with outsiders or only shared simple questions for symbolic purposes. (The study found that about one-third of the studied members resisted the new approach.) Similarly, many of your top people's minds get offended and worried if you propose opening up your business for outside expertise.

Source: Lifshitz-Assaf, 2018

Another example worth considering is a department store that would benefit from creating an e-commerce platform. In the best case, it would integrate the brick and mortar operations seamlessly into online operations. However, employees at the department store might actively rebel against online operations. They fear losing their jobs as commerce moves online. Therefore, many traditional successful companies failed in the transition to e-commerce, and newcomers won.

Four steps to turn organizational fear into energy

You don't need to be afraid of organization rigidity and resistance. There are simple steps you can take to turn them into a powerful force of change.

Four steps to turn organizational fear into energy:

1 Involve members of the organization in the option creation and evaluation

2 Emphasize continuity in communication

3 Support and enable learning

4 Use internal analytics to optimize your timing

---

1. Involve members of the organization in the option creation and evaluation

A portion of organization members' worries about becoming an intelligent platform comes from a lack of knowledge and understanding. Either they are not aware of the external trends and forces that force your organization to become a platform. Or they have formed suspicious ideas of your true motives for the change. Hence, the more you can involve them in the actual strategic thinking process, the less they will fear.

You can involve your organization members in every step of the process described above to reduce executive fear. You can do this in a sufficiently light way, such that you do not slow down the process too much or risk leaking sensitive information. Still, when people are part of the process, they can undergo the same emotional and cognitive growth as executives. They will experience this even if they are not part of the final decision-making or do not have access to all options and data.

In practice, many organizations that we have worked with have used the following kinds of approaches:

a Communicate early on in the process that the purpose is to investigate the strategic situation and consider many options. Hence, all ideas and perspectives are welcome. This communication creates psychological safety.

b Share information about the external trends and competitive situation in internal presentations and other appropriate forums. You can also ask them to contribute to SWOT-analyses. Remind people that it is beneficial for everyone to understand the reality before jumping to conclusions. In this way, you enhance mindfulness.

c Invite people to generate and suggest potential platforms and other strategic options for your firm. You can do this in workshops or via online channels. As they see many options shared by their colleagues, they understand that their idea is not the only potential direction and become more open to change.

d Organize debates and other critical workshops and online surveys to identify the essential assumptions for each strategic option. In this way, you further help your organization members see the strategic situation's complexity and let go of their old, rigid beliefs that contribute to their resistance.

e Ask them to develop potential action plans for a select number of options. They imagine the actions. Therefore, they become more accustomed to taking them, reducing the shock effect that could generate resistance.

2. Emphasize continuity in communication

In any radical change, it is the change that generates fear. Hence, rather than emphasizing the amount of change in your communication, it is often beneficial to emphasize those things that do NOT change. You generate a feeling of continuity, which makes people feel safe. Even though some new stuff will happen, most activities will stay the same. Hence, the platform strategy is not that scary, after all. Instead, the novel aspects can start feeling exciting.

Netflix had a mail-in DVD business when streaming emerged as a new business model. It saw the opportunity early on. The CEO had outlined a long-term vision. It was only a matter of time when the computing power and connectivity would be adequate to make the transition. Netflix had started the transformation by changing its business model for DVDs from single rental to subscription. Thus, the introduction of streaming was not a radical change. It was continuity of the current business.

After it had divested its phone business to Microsoft, Nokia used this approach. It was a radical strategic change for the company. In its communication, Nokia emphasized its 150-year-long history and how it had renewed itself multiple times. The term 'Change DNA' was created. Employees did not feel sad about losing the mobile phone identity. Instead, there was pride in the more abstract identity of changing and renewing.

In NASA's case, identity work created continuity (Lifshitz-Assaf, 2018). Many company engineers started reframing their work as solution seekers rather than problem solvers. They had always found solutions to the most challenging and essential problems related to space travel. Traditionally, they had spent much time searching for the solution internally. In contrast, after the change, they also explored alternatives from outside the company. Hence, even though their activities changed, they did not change that radically. Therefore, they felt less threatened.

3. Support and enable learning

Once you start implementing a platform business model and AI-based learning loops, your employees need to start acting in new ways. New processes require learning many new things. Moving from controlling your supply chain to orchestrating partners might be challenging. Interacting with an AI software can be difficult. Employees feel 'learning anxiety', ie stress and feelings of being unable to perform what the company and their colleagues expect. If this anxiety gets very high, people can become rigid in their behaviours, actively resist the new requirements or leave your organization.

But avoid responding by increasing pressure for employees. Instead, seek to reduce the learning anxiety in the organization. The problem is not that employees do not want to learn (in which case pressure would motivate them). The problem is they feel they cannot. To reduce learning anxiety, you should support and enable learning in multiple ways.

A good practice is to balance learning needs with support. Focus on the necessary skills. Ideally, you can do this in increments. Employees can learn a subset of the skills, take them into practice, routinize them and then learn a new subset of skills.

Companies and their employees need to become more AI literate. Therefore, they require education and training. An excellent example is E.ON, a German energy company. It made a specific effort to increase data and AI literacy in the company. Hence, it organized training on visualizing and interacting with data from inside and outside the company. Also, it commissioned nano-degrees from Udacity in machine learning, computer vision and deep reinforcement learning (Insead, 2020).

With a proper understanding of AI, E.ON defined value pools to see the most significant AI opportunities. For example, smart assets and networks and AI-assisted energy economics. AI is not about technology but driving tangible value.

In addition to helping employees master new skills, you need to help them understand the new business model's logic. Employees often do not see an intelligent platform's overall value that optimizes performance on a system level. Employees can see only part of the system. Therefore, they might feel that the required actions from them are unnecessary or even harmful. For example, they might think the need to log in more information about customers and their activities might be wasteful. They cannot see how this information is beneficial for other operations in the organization.

To avoid an adverse reaction to system-level optimization, you need to show how various elements are linked together in space and time. Understanding the bigger picture allows employees to know how their use of AI and platform tools helps the organization. It also helps if you align incentives with the new goal of optimizing a larger picture. You should reward employees for behaviours that benefit the AI and platform use, not only local results.

4. Use internal analytics to optimize your timing

Communication is most effective when it is customized to match the mood and preferences of the target. Traditionally, organizational change communication has relied on middle managers to customize the CEO message to their employees. In contrast, CEO communication has remained generic. However, nowadays, AI and other tools enable leaders to target their communication far more effectively.

For example, you can collect data on employees' day-to-day feelings and attitudes with Moodmetric or similar tools. On some days, they are enthusiastic and motivated, whereas on others, their mood is gloomy. You could use such data to determine whether an individual is exceptionally responsive to changes made on a particular day. Thus, you can choose the optimal timing of change communication and actions. For example, you could create a one-week period during which you will communicate specific changes. A more-positive-than-average daily mood by employees would trigger communication.

Very often, management struggles with tracking change projects. Project management offices try to keep up with schedules, risks and changes. Now, AI-powered project management tools are emerging.

AI tracks teams and individuals' relative progress in a change programme and customizes the change actions and communication accordingly. For example, some individuals or groups have adopted most of the new behaviours required for the change initiative. They are more likely to appreciate positive communication focused on the next round of changes and future challenges. In contrast, some individuals and groups struggle with the earlier steps. They might be better motivated by additional support resources, the provision of structure, managers' willingness to acknowledge the adverse effect and other types of support.

Predictive analytics would allow you to manage change projects on a more proactive basis (Stenius and Vuori, 2018). You could systematically anticipate impediments and obstacles, potentially even before they affect the work environment. For example, coffee breaks might take a few minutes longer than before, as measured via employee computer activity. Or there might be increased traffic on websites not related to work. These might be early warning signals of reduced motivation during change implementation. If you identify such signs, you can revise your action plans and communication to address problems that might not have fully emerged or become apparent.

Partners' fear: scepticism and distrust

When you are creating an intelligent platform, you need users and other companies to join. Having them is crucial because network effects are the driver of value in platforms. Furthermore, to maximize continuous improvement with AI-enabled learning loops, you need data from as many partners as possible. However, potential partners' leaders may fear that the platform will not succeed despite significant investment or that you will exploit them and reap all the benefits.

For example, B2B platforms need to attract both the demand and supply sides to join. When Tetrapak launched its B2B spare parts and service marketplace, it had to convince third-party suppliers to join.

Even if leaders are confident that a particular platform will be successful, they may distrust the platform's owner. They perceive that they could join the winning platform, but they would not benefit enough from it. They think other members of the platform would benefit from their joining more than they would.

For example, Nokia faced a big dilemma in 2010, when it had to decide between Android and Windows as a new platform for its smartphones. Android had the highest market share. It would have been a safe bet in the sense that at least Nokia would join a successful platform. In contrast, Windows had a much smaller market share and no certainty whether it would become mainstream.

However, while many outsiders thought Android would be the obvious choice, it did not look similar to Nokia. If Nokia joined the Android platform, it would have to accept the platform's rules. Nokia did not perceive these to be attractive. In particular, Google was gaining profits from the application ecosystem operating via the platform. Besides, Google treated each company in the Android ecosystem equally. It reduced them to the role of a hardware designer who uses (roughly) the same operating system as every competitor. Hence, Nokia leaders worried that the Android ecosystem's competition would squeeze their profits and that only Google would benefit from Nokia's joining in. Therefore, Nokia chose Windows. But the Windows ecosystem never took off.

Trust toward the partners is particularly important when extensive data sharing is needed to accelerate AI use. However, companies often find it highly troublesome to share their data with other companies. For example, a company developing a predictive maintenance solution for factories had difficulties getting access to the required data. Its customers thought that sharing their data would benefit their competitors. Or that the platform would get into a too-strong position.

Turn partners' fear into energy through these steps

You can take several actions to turn your partners' fear into energy. In this way, their fear does not need to create friction but energize your joint efforts and boost the platform's success.

Four steps to turn partners' fear into energy:

1 Initiate relationship building as early as possible

2 Communicate a clear vision with members already on board

3 Generate positive emotional experiences

4 Maintain momentum through frequent joint actions, even if small

---

1. Initiate relationship building as early as possible

People are sceptical toward strangers with a proposal – often for a good reason. Thus, you should make sure that you are no stranger when you start negotiating about a collaboration with a potential partner firm. You can make yourself known in multiple ways, as found by Stanford University research on the successful ventures in Silicon Valley:

a Communicate actively about your leadership and share stories (Santos and Eisenhardt, 2009). The more visible you are in an area, the more people get familiar with your face (or company logo). Psychological research calls this 'the mere exposure effect'. People start trusting people and entities they frequently see, even if they had no interactions or further knowledge. Biologically, this makes sense, as every encounter without an attack is evidence of you not being a predator.

b Ask for help and mentoring long before making a proposal. One of the most striking findings has been that companies who ask for help and mentoring early on are perceived more positively than others. People are flattered when someone asks for advice from them. And the flattery generates positive emotion, which gets associated with the person asking for advice (Hallen and Eisenhardt, 2012).

2. Communicate a clear vision with members already on board

There are other reasons for other companies not joining your intelligent platform. For instance, they might believe the platform will fail. You can reduce this feeling by showing a compelling vision. Also, a large number of firms that have already joined amplifies the impression of success.

Research performed at Stanford University by Pinar Ozcan and Kathleen Eisenhardt (2009) showed how proactive and courageous communication helps companies successfully build alliances. These companies envision a winning network and industry structure. Then they sell their vision to persuade multiple partners at once. They make it look like their innovation is succeeding by ensuring that other companies are already on board. They say to every company they meet: 'look, all the others are already with us', which makes them join. Thus, the promise becomes a reality, and they gain a critical mass of supporting companies.

In contrast, less successful firms approach potential partner firms one by one without communicating a clear vision of what they are building. The potential partners are thus less likely to perceive that the platform will succeed. Therefore, they are less likely to join, and the platform becomes less likely to succeed.

In 2020, Amazon's logo change communicated its big vision. The arrow from a to z signalled that you could get everything from Amazon. It was confident. Amazon convinced even its competitors to join in by boosting their short-term revenue. Brands like ToysRUs, Borders and Target lined up. Also, it attracted smaller third-party sellers by promising to share analytics (Kelion, 2020).

3. Generate positive emotional experiences

When people experience positive emotions with someone, they come to associate these emotions with that someone. Hence, if you can make your potential partners experience any positive emotion during interactions with you, they are more likely to feel favourable toward you. And their fear turns into energy for the collaboration.

CASE STUDY Generating positive emotions to motivate collaboration

Virta Ltd is a successful European start-up developing a charging ecosystem for electric vehicles.

During its founding years, the company co-founders, Jussi Palola and Elias Pöyry, met many potential partner firms and always sought to generate positive emotions and excitement toward electric cars and the company. They often started meetings with a test drive of an electric vehicle. They'd let the partner drive the car and sense its smoothness and acceleration. It was still early times for electric vehicles. Hence, for many, this was their first experience.

Consequently, they got highly excited. And this excitement became associated with potential collaboration (Vuori and Huy, 2016b).

Intentional generation of emotional excitement spurred the company's success. It was the first company in the charging industry to be included in *The Financial Times* FT 1000 list of the fastest-growing companies in 2020 (Virta, 2020). By 2021, the company is operating in 30 countries.

In addition to creating pleasant and exciting emotional experiences during its early years, Virta has systematically considered its partners' perspective. Virta's business model relies on local partners who install and own the charging stations. At the same time, Virta provides the platform for operating them. Virta seeks to excite and empower its partners by letting them have their brand visible. In this way, the partners can be proud of building the electric vehicle infrastructure while Virta operates in the background.

Furthermore, Virta has sought to make the process extremely smooth for its partners. Therefore, they can act immediately without any hassle or complications once a potential partner gets excited. Instead, they merely plug-in to Virta's solution that includes the business concept and key processes, technology and customer relationship management.

Apple, Google and other companies dependent on many external developers also seek to generate emotional excitement in various ways. The events organized by these companies include lots of humour and exciting presentation. 'There's one more thing' – the famous ending of Steve Jobs at Apple events. Steve Jobs turned dull product introductions into huge media spectacles.

They also share lots of free stuff (t-shirts and the like) that generates pleasant feelings and supports identification with the company. They also share more instrumental materials for free. For example, they open source AI and machine learning software to create trust and speed up innovation. Open sourcing helps create empathy towards customers and smaller developers (Forbes, 2019). One example of this is Google which open sourced Tensor Flow, a platform for machine learning implementations.

4. Maintain momentum through frequent joint actions, even if small

Intelligent platforms thrive from structured interaction between various parties. If you meet once, you have contact. If you do a joint project, you have a good start. To create a functioning platform, you need repeated interaction.

Therefore, you should create various activities in which you and your partner firms jointly create something. These can be relatively simple things like joint marketing efforts or co-developing a feature. Each interaction pulls the parties together and reinforces links between them. As a result, they get used to working with one another. Thus, they spontaneously start thinking of one another as partners. As they do so, they start investing evermore in the partnership.

For example, Google has a large ecosystem of developers who do not work for Google but use Google's products and contribute to their development. To keep these individuals hooked into the system, Google organizes various local and global events for them, in addition to frequent online communication. By doing so, Google frequently creates interactions that reinforce the individuals' identification with Google and its ecosystem, making them even more committed to it. It also inspires new ideas on what they could do with and for Google tools. As a result, the likelihood that they will remain in the Google ecosystem increases.

Key takeaways for your organization

Fear can prevent your strategic transformation into an intelligent platform. People experience fear because the platform logic and the use of AI contain uncertainties, challenge old assumptions, reduce their sense of control and threaten their identities. Executives' fear causes organizations to paralyse or panic. Organizational fear causes rigidity and resistance. Partners' fear causes them not to join your platform. Their fear is manifest as scepticism and distrust.

However, fear does not have to stop you. Reflect on the following questions. They will help you recognize the fears lurking in your organization and turn them into energy.

Executive fear

- How do platform business models and AI challenge your executive team's current assumptions and identity? How does that make you and your team members feel?
- How could you make discussions between executives feel safe to bring up any perspectives and get excited about novel prospects?
- What options could you create for becoming a platform and adopting AI? What would be the most exciting aspects of each?
- For each option, could you consider the first steps and approach potential partners?

Organizational fear

- What signs of fear, rigidity and resistance related to platforms and AI has your organization displayed?
- How could the members of your organization contribute to option creation and evaluation?

- How could you support learning in your organization? How could you communicate what current skills and activities will also remain valuable in the future?
- Do you know when the members of your organization feel demotivated and when they get excited? How could you better track their feelings in real time?

Partners' fear

- What worries and doubts do your potential partner firms have about your platform?
- Have you initiated informal trust building with potential partners?
- How could you communicate your leadership and vision? How could you make potential partners feel the excitement and other positive emotions?
- How can you keep up and speed up momentum with those partners who have already shown interest?

CHAPTER TWO

Remove friction

The nail gun was singing as Tom constructed the wooden frame for a new house. Then, the gun went silent. It turns out it's broken. 'On no, it's going to take time and effort to get a new one', Tom thought.

But, no worries, Power tool giant Hilti's fleet management delivers a new tool in a matter of hours. As the nail gun has a communication chip inside, it can be easily identified and localized. Thus, getting a broken tool replaced is a frictionless experience. There is no need to be anxious about broken tools; no need to spend time searching for a replacement. In the future, AI could even predictively schedule tool repairs before breakdowns while delivering the right replacements straight to workers at the construction site.

Our research shows that successful platforms started from identifying industries and processes that had high friction. Platform companies focused on removing this friction to reduce transaction costs (Laukia, 2018) Leinonen, 2020; Mohn, 2017; Repo, 2018). Removing friction makes services easier to access, unlocks new value and disrupts incumbents.

Hilti is an example of early movers in creating frictionless experiences. Already in 2000, it launched Hilti Fleet Management for premium power tools in the construction industry. Instead of buying tools, customers paid a monthly fee to access equipment, with fast repairs available, and trackage of tool usage, ensuring fewer breakdowns.

Hilti's fleet management service reduces transaction costs. Transaction costs refer to money, time and effort exerted for purchasing or using your product or service. A search for the right tool takes less time than before, and less effort is required to get it delivered. The customer has peace of mind as they know that valuable time is not lost when tools break and need reparation. And Hilti can track the tools' usage to ensure proper handling.

In this chapter, we will discuss how platforms emerge as they remove friction. Reducing transaction costs eliminates friction. If transaction costs are too high, your customers will not purchase your product or service. It is just too much of an effort to buy, even if they love the product and the price.

We will cover three types of transaction costs:

- search and effort costs;
- uncertainty and anxiety costs;
- opportunism-related costs.

We will outline concepts and processes to address these. We will also demonstrate how intelligent platforms learn from data to reduce friction. Finally, we will explain how intelligent platforms address these three costs together, creating frictionless experiences. With this approach, intelligent platforms create magic, raise the bar for user experience and disrupt industries.

Friction creates opportunities

Friction manifests itself as transaction costs. A transaction cost is any cost involved in making an economic transaction (Rindfleisch, 2020; Williamson, 2017). For example, when shipping cargo there will be some transaction costs in addition to the price of the shipping itself. Transaction costs can be monetary, such as the commission of booking a truck through an intermediary company, or more abstract such as time and mental effort required for performing the transaction.

Transaction costs are a general concept. However, their role is significant in platform businesses for two reasons. First, platforms often gain an advantage over other companies because the platform model can substantially reduce transaction costs. Therefore, they enable a more efficient organization. Think of how Uber disrupted inefficient taxi companies. A taxi ride is now one click away, and you have peace of mind as you see what type of vehicle and driver you get and when exactly it will arrive. Or how Airbnb created a whole new market by connecting homeowners and travellers.

Second, creating smooth transactions can be a critical step in reaching the critical mass of customers you need for successfully launching a platform. Simple onboarding of new customers is essential for platforms. If your customer needs to type too much, wait too long or are uncertain what they have just signed up for, you have lost the game. Other services provide a faster and more convenient experience.

Many industries have an established way of doing things which is part of the industry's conventional wisdom. We know things are not optimal, but we accept the status quo. Until somebody does not and changes everything, like the fate of Blockbuster. Renting DVDs in a store was fine until it wasn't. Netflix created a frictionless experience to watch your favourite movie. The change in customer expectation platforms started in B2C, but now we see many B2B businesses getting disrupted. And the Covid-19 crisis has accelerated the pace of change.

To succeed with your platform, you need a step-change in customer experience. For example, there was high friction in offline commerce in China as the credit card system was not as developed as in western countries. To remove this friction, Ant Financial introduced Alipay QR code payments. Consumers paid by scanning a QR code provided by the merchant. Ant Financial took its first step towards a platform.

Already early on, Amazon realized it needed to reduce friction from e-commerce. It took too long to get the purchased goods. Therefore, it launched Amazon Prime with two-day or even same-day delivery.

Intelligent platforms don't settle for a one-off reduction in friction. They reduce friction continuously by learning from data. Your next Uber drive is faster than the previous as the company's tracking and mapping capabilities improve. Also, your Uber driver is better than the last due to constant feedback.

Buzzwords such as blockchain, AI, IoT (Internet of Things), RFID (radio-frequency identification), drones, robotics and AR/VR (augmented reality/ virtual reality), to name a few, are hyped as capable of disrupting every business. Companies and their leaders focus on developing a specific technology in-house, acquiring it, or investing in start-ups. Very often, this leads to inflated expectations of the change. And after a few proof-of-concept projects, the initial enthusiasm dies down, and attention moves to the next technology.

But if you view the new technology as an enabler to reduce friction, you are onto something. Think about how Netflix identified connectivity and computing power as enablers for streaming. They waited for the right moment to exploit them to deliver their service.

Inexpensive RFID tags enable the identification and tracking of physical products. Digital data encoded into RFIF tags, also referred to as smart labels, can be read via radio waves. For instance, RFID tags identify Hilti power tools. Thus, Hilti can track power tool usage in real time and anticipate each phase of construction's required tools. They can thus proactively create a tool plan for a construction site and optimize assets by allocating the right equipment in the right place at the right time.

Drones reduce friction in accessing information. Previously, you needed a helicopter to take aerial photos and video. Now you can use drones to survey crops, fields, forests, oil pipes, windmills and other critical infrastructure. There is less effort and fewer costs. Furthermore, data creates a network effect. Every new customer brings new data that trains AI models. And therefore, AI models continuously improve how they predict breakdowns.

Technology makes things faster and more straightforward. It eliminates middle-men and brings new assets to the network. All of this reduces transaction costs, and that drives success with platforms.

Next, we will discuss each type of transaction costs in detail and what you should do to reduce and eliminate them.

Search and effort costs

Imagine you are an engineer fixing a faulty machine in a yacht factory. The device is roaring, and you locate the problem to be a broken hydraulic pump. Unfortunately, you don't have a spare one on site. Furthermore, the company manufacturing the pump went bankrupt a couple of years ago, and the pump is no longer available in your typical spare-part channels.

You need a corresponding pump. And you need it quickly, as every hour the machine is not running costs US $20,000 in lost sales and fixed costs. You try googling hydraulic pumps. You find several, but none of the websites tell you if their pump can substitute your pump. They also do not provide accurate information about delivery times.

You start calling the companies to get additional information. Someone picks up the phone in the first company. Next, they transfer you to another person. This person tells you their pumps are incompatible. In the second company, the person reviews manuals and ultimately explains to you it won't work. The operation has already taken three hours, costing your company US $60,000.

Finally, the third company tell you that the pump will probably suit your needs. You're relieved. But there's a catch. The company stores the pumps in a warehouse where only one employee has enough training to recognize the right pump. And they are on medical leave. You, therefore, need to drive to the warehouse yourself to identify and pick up the pump. It's 200 miles – another three hours each way. The total cost of the machine not running is reaching nearly US $200,000. Besides, you have wasted a full working day searching for the part and then driving to get it.

This example illustrates what we call search and effort costs. They are costs that your customers incur to find and acquire your product or service. They will repel your customers even if they like your product.

Search costs occur when the desired product or service is not readily available. In such situations, one first needs to search for a provider for the service or the product, and this search process can take plenty of time and money. For example, when one wants to find a new expert employee on a critical task, it often takes several weeks of active efforts to find suitable candidates. This search cost occurs before the actual transaction to form the employment contract even begins.

Effort costs refer to costs that occur due to performing the transaction. They can include, for example, the travel needed to the store for purchasing the product or the clicks and typing required before being able to stream online content.

When the transaction cost is high compared to the value of the product or service, it is more likely to influence whether one buys the product or service. For example, suppose a taxi ride to a restaurant costs US $20 each way. In comparison, a nice (but not luxurious) meal costs only US $30. In that case, the transaction cost is higher than the price of the meal you want to have. Therefore, you might choose not to purchase the meal because it is too expensive to get the meal relative to the pleasure and nutrition the meal will provide. Another example is when buying a mobile game requires a complicated login and several clicks; the transaction effort ends up being too high compared to the pleasure the game would give you, so you never buy it.

Minimize search and effort costs with these steps

Search and effort costs can make it too difficult for your customers to use your platform, even if they love it. The total cost for customers is not only the money they directly pay. It also includes the effort they need to exert to get to you and the additional fees related to that effort. To maximize customer engagement, you need to minimize this extra friction. The following steps guide you.

Five steps to minimize search and effort costs in your platform

1 Consolidate demand and supply with a marketplace

2 Create intelligent matchmaking

3 Minimize the number of decisions for customers

4 Enable access to unused assets and reduce the need for capital

5 Use technology to automate and smooth the experience

---

1. Consolidate demand and supply with a marketplace

A marketplace is a platform for buyers and sellers to meet and do trade. Traditional marketplaces were on town squares, but nowadays digital approaches have increased convenience, speed and scale. Digital marketplaces consolidate demand and supply in fragmented industries and reduce search and effort costs, like Amazon and Alibaba. Marketplaces have given birth to new markets like Airbnb by connecting homeowners and travellers.

Consumers drove the first wave of marketplaces. However, the same phenomena are behind B2B marketplaces. Business users also expect a simple user experience such as they have become used to with B2C services. Therefore, consolidating demand and supply with a marketplace provides ample business opportunities.

Tetra Pak provides solutions and services for the food and beverage industry. In 2019, it launched a B2B marketplace for spare parts and consumables. Tetra Pak has provided equipment for 5,000 factories around the world. A large number of suppliers offer spare parts and consumables. Hence, factories face a problem with coordination. There is no central place to make an order. That's why Tetra Pak innovated for a better solution.

Tetra Pak is one of the biggest suppliers to their customers. However, customers buy things from others as well. But customers would like to have a one-stop shop. Tetra Pak B2B Marketplace drives speed, convenience and transparency. In the marketplace model, Tetra Pak does not hold stock of the marketplace. Instead, the original seller keeps these orders. They are shipped on demand directly to customers. And Tetra Pak monitors them in terms of service level.

2. Create intelligent matchmaking

Making supply and demand meet has been one of the central economic challenges throughout humankind's history. You have people with a solution and others with a problem – but most often, these two people don't know about one another. Traditionally, they have found one another by chance in places like open square markets or service-specific locations such as taxi stands.

As digital marketplaces emerge, more intelligent matchmaking can significantly reduce search costs. We can communicate what we need and what we can offer. And networked software algorithms find matches for us.

Intelligent matchmaking can indeed be intelligent, meaning that algorithms can identify compatibility between a need and a solution using data without active customer involvement.

With Upwork, people or companies can easily hire a freelancer. Or you can become one, offer your services and start earning money. We call it the gig economy. The platform's algorithms enable fast matchmaking between employers and employees, reducing the search cost associated with finding the right person for the job. With a rating system, the best ones get differentiated. As a result, friction and thus search costs are reduced.

To make your intelligent matchmaking, you need to start by reflecting on the matchmaking challenges faced by prospective platform clients. Consider what services or products a particular group of people or companies need. Then, evaluate how easy or difficult it is to find and use the service or product when required. In those areas where they find it most difficult, your platform might improve matchmaking.

But you also need to consider the other side: what services and products do companies offer. How do they find their clients? Do they need to find more customers in a less effortful way? Again, if the supplier of a service or product faces friction in the selling process, your platform could improve the situation.

Having recognized both potential consumers of a product or service and a supplier, you need to reflect on what creates an excellent match. What parameters can you measure to predict if a particular client will benefit from a specific supplier and if the supplier will consider the transaction attractive?

CASE STUDY Intelligent matching for elderly well-being

To illustrate intelligent matchmaking, consider Gubbe – a Finnish start-up providing well-being services for the elderly. The company founders recognized that older people would benefit from regular interaction with other people. Such meetings would improve their cognitive functioning, emotional well-being and physical health. However, many older people live far away from their close relatives. They have a limited number of friends who are often immobile. Hence, they are often lonely. They have a need, and high friction is preventing them from having the need satisfied.

On the other hand, young adults generally want to experience their life as more meaningful. They might lack significant inter-generational interaction due to having moved to study or work in a new city. Also, they might need extra cash. Helping the elderly might, therefore, bring them both psychological and economic benefits. However, finding a place for volunteer work is often not easy. For example, they might have to commit to a specific shelter or event. Hence, they have a desire to help the elderly, but friction is limiting them.

Gubbe created a matchmaking platform for the elderly and young adults. Via the platform, the older person's relatives (on behalf of the elder) invite a young person to accompany the more senior person; for example, playing games or going for a walk. The young person can sign up as a volunteer and get invited. Gubbe considers several carefully selected parameters and the elderly and the young persons' locations to ensure safe and suitable matches.

You can also apply intelligent matchmaking in B2B business. For example, a spare parts marketplace could maintain factory configurations of clients. Therefore, it knows the necessary parts and can use additional parameters to make the best match for parts and service. B2B marketplaces are not generic e-commerce sites but much more intelligent platforms. They simplify processes, reduce the need for repeating what's already known and reduce search and effort costs.

AI further improves intelligent matchmaking, creating a learning loop. Each matchmaking produces new data that can be used to train and improve AI algorithms. We will discuss the learning loop more in detail in Chapter 4.

3. Minimize the number of decisions for customers

Once a customer has chosen your product, they want the product without additional hassle. Yet, many companies still require their prospective buyers to consider various options or details before completing the transaction.

Often, these additional considerations take a substantial amount of time from the customer. They need to think the choices through while they have limited background knowledge required for making these choices.

To reduce the customer effort needed, offer a default option that is likely suitable for most customers.

CASE STUDY   Minimizing decisions in the e-car charging solutions

Several energy companies, facility owners and other stakeholders are interested in having charging stations for electric cars. However, creating a station requires making several choices. These choices include several technical decisions related to the charging solution, the customer experience during the charging, the business model and process for operating the charging, the installation process and many others. If you are a busy manager, it gets overwhelming. You are likely to return to more urgent tasks instead of studying the specifics to make the right choices.

To minimize friction in charging station operation, Virta Ltd created an analogous solution to Amazon's one-click shopping. As a facility or other stakeholder representative, you can contact Virta, and they will provide you a ready package. They organize the installation and put your logo on the equipment visible to the customer. Hence, without friction, you have your own charging station.

At the same time, Virta offers solutions for electric car drivers to use the charging stations easily. In this way, Virta connects the facility or energy company with drivers of electric cars with minimal friction.

To minimize the number of decisions your customers need to take, follow these principles:

- Simple first use: require minimum information in the sign-up for service, reduce all unnecessary steps.
- Get rid of feature creep: stop developing 2.0 when you can sell version 1.0.
- Instead of offering a large number of features, stick to a few essentials to gain critical mass.

Fewer choices are crucial at the beginning of your platform launch, as we discuss in Chapter 3.

4. Enable access to unused assets and reduce the need for capital

The world is moving to a sharing economy. Cars are unused 95 per cent of the time (Morris, 2016). Uber enabled the use of regular standard vehicles for taxi service. Airbnb realized that people have idle real estate that travellers could use. Uber and many other identified idle assets and intelligent ways of getting them used. Thus, they removed friction from leveraging assets that were not readily available for the ones needing them.

The brilliance of Uber, Airbnb and other sharing economy forerunners comes from a simple insight. They can increase the utilization of critical assets. In this way, those assets become (almost) free for the new service, as the platform does not need to purchase and own the assets. For example, Uber does not own the production assets, Uber drivers' private cars. Hence, it does not have to pay taxes, interests and maintenance fees for them. As the assets get (almost) free, there is no need to worry about additional capital.

Your platform can likewise reduce friction in people's life by enabling the use of under-used assets. For your customers, consider what assets they occasionally need to use but frequently own. Is there a way to facilitate sharing those assets via your platform? Alternatively, are similar assets being under-used in some other context? Could your platform facilitate the flexible use of those assets across the two domains?

Sometimes it is not possible to identify unused assets. Still, people don't want to or cannot afford to own things. Many markets are created by somebody taking the risk of ownership and lowering initial capital for customers. For example, Hilti moved from product sales into tool fleet leasing, maintenance and management-as-a-service.

By reducing the need for capital, you lower the barrier to try new things. Think of e-scooters. It is hard to move in cities: a car gets stuck in traffic, a bike is cumbersome and walking is too slow. E-scooters provided a convenient solution, available everywhere. You can pick them up anywhere and leave them anywhere; just pay with a mobile app.

Lightweight, powerful electric motors and advances in battery technology development made e-scooters possible. However, only a full-fledged ride-sharing platform, such as Tier, Voi or Lime, just to name a few, made e-scooters very popular and created a new business. The solution removed the friction of taking e-scooters into use and moving from one place to another. No need to spend an effort to find a store and have enough money to buy one. Less search and effort costs.

5. Use technology to automate and smooth the experience

For every point of friction, there might be a technological solution to reduce friction. Technology can smooth the transaction by requiring less manual or cognitive work (eg Schmidt and Wagner, 2019). You need to identify the friction points in your service or product and then consider how alternative technologies could smooth the transaction.

For example, Deliveroo, Wolt, DeliveryHero and Just Eat are all food delivery services. They eliminate friction from the experience of ordering food from your home sofa. They focus on how to make it easy to order online and deliver to your home. They use mobile internet and GPS to track and optimize delivery routes, enabling this seamless service. They eliminated friction from the process. AI is helping these companies to optimize operations even further.

Technology has smoothed transactions also in the financial industry. Buying a house is cumbersome, even when you have found a great home and are ready to close the deal. You still need to visit a bank to sign the paperwork, and this typically needs to happen at the same time as the seller signs.

A Finnish start-up, DIAS, executes real estate transactions for home-owners entirely digitally. DIAS uses a blockchain that stores information in a distributed manner in the databases of trading banks. This approach increases the safety and reliability of the platform. The buyer and seller can separately approve the deal without visiting a bank branch. The bank then transfers the money, and the system records the transaction.

Indian start-up Paytm offers services like mobile recharges, utility bill payments, travel, movies, events bookings and in-store payments. It uses a QR code. A QR code, short for quick response, is a two-dimensional barcode. It is a straightforward payment method as one needs only to generate a barcode and print it on a sign. Customers can then scan the code and pay with their mobile devices.

But QR codes also prove that focusing on technology is not enough to remove friction. One still needs to consider the whole value chain and consumer behaviour. In China and India, QR codes are widely adopted for payments, but they have not become popular in the western world. The difference might be cultural but also could be related to the status of the ecosystem. In western countries, merchants already had the necessary infrastructure for card payments, while they did not have them in India and China. QR code offered a convenient, cashless payment method without the need for upfront investment for card payment infrastructure.

John Deere is a pioneer in digitizing agriculture. Its IoT platform connects tractors, harvesters, planting, seeding and tillage equipment with the cloud. Furthermore, it collects and cultivates data for customer value. And based on these insights, the system commands equipment in the field. Ten-ton trucks can move with a precision that is second to none. Farmers share the data with suppliers for seeds, fertilizers and chemicals. Before these run out, an automatic order is triggered. Less effort cost.

With machine data, John Deere can predict problems with machines. Predictive maintenance looks at patterns in the data to identify faults. Technicians save time and effort, and there is less downtime for machines.

Augmented reality (AR) adds digital elements to a live view using the camera on a smartphone or AR glasses. For example, it can show a disassembly overlay on factory equipment, with step-by-step repair instructions. AR enhances the efficiency of the maintenance processes. Even a less skilled technician can perform maintenance work helped by the overlay or advice from a remote expert.

Sometimes new technology does not reduce friction but increases it. Take 3D. In the early 2010s, 3D TV was poised for a breakthrough. At Las Vegas Consumer Electronics Show, manufacturers touted 3D as the next disruption. However, there was little content available, and 3D glasses were hard to use. There was no friction 3D would eliminate. It created new friction as it was hard to acquire suitable content, and, thus, the overall value created for the consumers was too low. In a few years, 3D TV went from boom to bust, and in 2016 no Samsung TV had the 3D feature (Katzmaier, 2016).

Simple is beautiful and efficient. Amazon Dash Button is preconfigured to order specific products. Just press a button, and it triggers an automatic order – no need to type in anything into the system. Now Amazon has moved to virtual Dash Buttons that can be created for any frequently ordered products. It cuts effort costs and thus strengthens Amazon's platform appeal.

Consider the friction points experienced by the customers and other potential platform participants for your business. Where do they need to travel, input information or otherwise exert effort to purchase your product or service? For every manual effort, how might you use technology to remove or minimize the effort needed?

To identify taken-for-granted assumptions, challenge yourself to cut the transaction cost and time by 80 per cent. If it currently takes seven minutes for your customer to purchase your product, how could you cut that time to 84 seconds? If they now need to type in 200 characters to place the order, how could you reduce that down to 40 characters?

Similarly, for other potential platform partners, where do they experience friction, and how could you leverage technology to minimize this friction? If your partner currently needs to spend 10 hours revising their code for every app they want to use in your platform, how could you cut that down to 2 hours? If it takes 10 minutes per product to describe it on your platform, how could you slash that down to 2 minutes? If it takes 2 hours to adjust equipment to your machine needs, how could you cut that down to 24 minutes? If it takes an hour to train every new employee for your platform, how can you cut that down to 12 minutes?

Uncertainty and anxiety costs

Imagine again. You are the engineer looking for the hydraulic pump. But in this scenario, the third company representative says they can send you the pump immediately by taxi. The person on the phone takes your address and says, 'I will go pick it up right now and put it in a taxi'. Then you both say 'cheers!' and hang up.

You go to the bathroom and start wondering if they really found the right pump and shipped it already. Probably they will text you once it's in a taxi. But, after 15 minutes, still no text. You decide to call again. No answer. Probably they shipped it and went to a meeting. Or maybe they are still in the warehouse looking for it?

After an hour, you still don't know if the pump is on its way. But you do know everyone is waiting. You wonder if you should try yet another company. Order a second pump, just to be sure.

After 3 hours and 20 minutes, the taxi finally arrives. It's the right pump. You are relieved and run to install it. But the anxiety you've experienced during the past three hours makes you swear you will never use the same company again.

Uncertainty and anxiety costs refer to the mental and emotional toll related to the purchase and use of a particular service or product. This mental toll occurs between a purchase decision and the initiation and completion of the transaction. For example, after you order a taxi, there is typically a several-minute-long waiting period between placing the order and the taxi arriving. During this period, you are under uncertainty. It is not clear if the taxi is coming or not, and this uncertainty can generate anxiety, especially if you are in a hurry.

Minimize uncertainty and anxiety costs with these steps

People worry when they are waiting for their product or service. Uncertainty causes this worry, and it can turn into anxiety. If the concern is too severe, they will not continue doing business with your platform. Fortunately, there are several actions you can take to minimize the uncertainty and fear experienced by your platform members.

Four steps to minimize uncertainty and anxiety costs in your platform:

1 Provide real-time tracking

2 Use rich media for communication

3 Communicate planned actions and timeline

4 Build a reputation of reliability and trust

---

1. Provide real-time tracking

When you order a ride from Uber or a meal from Wolt, you immediately get to know how long it will take for your order to arrive. You also see the progress of your order, as the time to arrival steadily decreases. This information reassures you that the order is really on its way and no-one has forgotten you.

For you to develop relevant real-time tracking for your customers, you need to start from their perspective. What are the uncertainties and anxieties experienced by your customers and other platform members? To answer this question, think about what the customers experience after they have placed their order. You can simply imagine the process or simulate the transaction in a workshop. You might even interview several customers.

Do they get an immediate confirmation that you have received their order? Does the message simply automatically acknowledge the order has been entered in a system or does it provide additional, reassuring information?

How long does it take for the customer to receive their order? What updates and information do they receive during the waiting period? What happens if there are delays?

What kinds of information could you provide for them to reduce their anxiety in the different stages of the process?

2. Use rich media for communication

Anxiety stemming from uncertainty is an emotional reaction. As emotions are often irrational, providing facts is not enough. Instead, you need to communicate in ways that appeal to emotions.

Consider ordering a sandwich from Subway. Not only do you know that the employee prepares your sandwich, but it's made right under your eyes. You can be sure about every detail of the process. Do they put in the meat and vegetables you ordered? Do they leave out the items that give you an allergic reaction? As you can see everything, you can be confident. Subway's process is a perfect illustration of how visibility to the process removes your anxiety.

Virtual experience can give the same reassurance. Images, voice and other rich communication methods tell the story. Uber does not only tell you that your ride will arrive in three minutes, it shows you the car on a map. Seeing the car approaching makes you feel that it is getting closer – even though you are not learning new information about the estimated time of arrival. And Uber also shows the car's colour, which reduces the customer's uncertainty of spotting the right vehicle.

When shipping products, instead of just texting the customer that the product is now on its way, you could send them a picture of the shipped product. Even better, the image could 'travel' on a map towards the customer's location, based on real-time location data.

If you are manufacturing based on custom orders, you can send updates on the progress. For example, you could send the customer pictures of the order being prepared.

To get started, consider what images, videos or other rich media would most appeal to your customer.

3. Communicate planned actions and timeline

Anxiety partly stems from the customer not knowing 'how long is this supposed to take' or 'why are they now doing that'. You can remove this anxiety by communicating the actions you need to take, why you take them and how long it will take.

For example, when a customer has purchased goods from your website, you can communicate what happens next. Order is processed, packaged, delivered to shipping, what shipping option was used and how long the estimated delivery is.

4. Build a reputation of reliability and trust

Anxiety stems from the perception that you cannot be sure the seller fulfills your order or that the partner delivers what they promised. Your perception of their reliability and actions is partly based on their reputation. If they are known for always delivering, you feel less anxiety than if they lack such standing.

The impact of reputation can be partly subconscious and irrational. Research on various domains has shown how superficial characteristics, such as body weight, gender and ethnic background, substantially influence people's perceptions. In the business domain, brands have a similar non-conscious influence on people. We trust familiar brands more than unknown ones, even if they technically delivered the same results.

Within your platform, you can create mechanisms that increase the platform participants' perceptions of reliability. In various settings, sharing customer reviews is a powerful approach. When people see that many others have found the service or product trustworthy, they will also trust it. Often, a simple five-star rating is enough like the ones on Uber and Airbnb.

You can also increase your reputation by having certificates and external reviews. These provide evidence that your platform members are indeed doing what they promise.

You can also leverage more subconsciously appealing techniques. They include using symbols and images that people associate with reliability and trustworthiness. As they see the photos, their emotional reaction is reassuring, shaping their perception of the actual service or product provider positively.

In B2B services, a trustworthy company launching a new service can vet experts, thus providing a service guarantee. This approach can help kick-start the platform, and you can add third-party feedback as the platform matures.

Opportunism-related costs

People are not always honest. You agree and pay but never receive what was agreed. You deliver what was agreed but never receive the payment. The counterpart denies having agreed with you or simply disappears.

At other times, people do not directly cheat or lie. Still, they are opportunistic in another way: they exploit the close relationship they have formed with you. For example, you might confirm a close partnership with a particular component manufacturer. You end up changing your product design to match the component's unique characteristics. There might be other components with similar functionality but different shapes or other parameters. Hence, the component's supplier can charge extra from you: they know that you will not change the supplier because that would generate a considerable cost for you.

A third way for potential partners to behave opportunistically is to cut you out. Your platform might connect the provider and user of a service. As per the agreement, you get a percentage of the revenue as a fee for the platform services. However, the provider can suggest selling the service directly to the user without paying you anymore.

These three types of situations illustrate what leads to *opportunism-related costs*. They are costs that relate to ensuring that the transaction partner does what was agreed – ie countering the threat that the partner will behave opportunistically.

Platforms can reduce opportunism-related costs by leveraging data. For example, as Flexport handles thousands of transportations, they will ensure the quality of the service and, by using platform analytics, track that deliveries are made in time. Flexport will make sure that sent goods will reach the recipient following relevant laws, directives, regulations and contracts at the right time, right place and in a cost-effective manner. By digitizing the whole supply chain, it collects data and can detect any irregularities caused by a supplier cutting corners.

Minimize opportunism-related costs with these steps

People sometimes lie, steal or cheat. If this happens too often in your platform, your users lose their trust in the platform and go away. You should not let that happen. Use the following steps.

Four steps to minimize opportunism-related costs in your platform:

1 Eliminate bad behaviour with tracking and feedback

2 Provide feedback to all sides

3 Create transparency in the market

4 Imagine contingencies and create borders/rules/penalties and safeguards

1. Eliminate bad behaviour with tracking and feedback

Airbnb is reducing friction in listing your apartment or house. A key point here was also the creation of trust in reducing friction. The rating system (and insurance) created trust between the parties and thus reduced friction. For example, when people start to rent an apartment, they might still cancel at the last minute as they don't dare to make the payment. Or the owner won't list the apartment as they are afraid that strangers might destroy their property. By creating a simple rating system, you are building trust between parties.

Uber's rating system ranks not only drivers but also passengers. This creates trust that it's safe to drive and that badly behaving customers who harass drivers won't be tolerated. Both practices increase confidence in the system and thus drive further adoption of Uber. Furthermore, the system records the ride, and you can verify that the driver took the shortest route. It reduces the opportunity to cheat in an unfamiliar neighbourhood.

Upwork has a work monitoring system that records what the worker is doing. It creates trust that the worker spends the time you are paying for working and not doing other activities.

2. Provide feedback to all sides

Often, when we think of opportunism, we only consider the seller or provider of the service. However, it is equally possible for the customer to behave opportunistically. Customer opportunism is critical for platforms because they thrive from matchmaking and network effects. If platforms generate bad matches, they start losing suppliers, which leads to the loss of customers and an escalating vicious cycle.

Hence, the feedback you provide must go to all sides, like Uber reviews its customers. If a customer smokes in the car or yells at the driver, the driver will give the customer a low score. A low score makes it less likely that the same customer will get another ride. Hence, it incentivizes the customer to behave.

In your platform, consider how the customers could exploit the sellers. A generic approach of using a star rating is already sufficient for sharing customer reputation. If there are specific customer behaviours that harm sellers, you can also provide feedback on those behaviours.

3. Create transparency in the market

You could openly share price information on your platform, as Amazon does for third-party sellers, for example. Transparent information reduces customer perception that the seller is cheating them.

Maersk and IBM used blockchain for their joint venture Tradelens, a container logistics solution. It digitalizes the global shipping industry that is still very often run manually and with paper and pen. The Tradelens platform allows users to connect and share data. All parties get the same visibility to the trade, creating transparency.

4. Imagine contingencies and create borders/rules/penalties and safeguards

It's good to be optimistic and trust people – most of the time. However, to prevent opportunism, you need to think about how people might trick you or other users of your platform. You need not be in this mindset all the time, but it's good to reserve some time for paranoid thinking.

You could play a game where a select number of your team members seek to exploit the platform in different roles. As they come up with ideas, you should record those ideas down without judgement.

Once you have a list of potential ways to exploit your platform, you can start inventing ways to prevent such opportunistic behaviours. Sometimes you can define a rule; at other times, you might introduce additional checks.

However, you should avoid creating too many checks and balances, as they would make an additional layer of friction. That friction would prevent your platform from ever becoming successful.

One example of a sufficiently frictionless rule is to forbid the platform parties from transacting directly. The platform can explicitly prohibit the provider from selling to the consumer directly. Alternatively, when possible, the platform can prevent direct interaction between them by requiring them to communicate via the platform.

Airbnb uses another way to anticipate contingencies. Airbnb's Host Guarantee extends to US $1 million. If the customer damages the house, the owner is fully compensated up to US $1 million. Hence, the owners can feel safer about giving their home to strangers via Airbnb.

You need to balance between preventing bad things from happening and keeping the experience smooth for the platform's honest users and stakeholders. As a heuristic, you could consider the following kinds of threats: 1) frequent small opportunistic behaviours, such as your platform partner performing a portion of the work outside the platform, and 2) rare but disastrous behaviours, such as violent acts by platform partners toward customers. Then you need to consider which of the risks are so large that you have to mitigate them.

In defining the mitigation actions, it is crucial that you always consider the additional friction created by the mitigation. You should think of how you can achieve the same mitigation effectiveness with less friction. For example, suppose you can reduce the first supplier selling some of the services outside the platform via AI algorithms that detect anomalies. In that case, this creates far less friction than routinely interrogating the customers. Likewise, non-intrusive surveillance could, in some situations, reduce the risk of more harmful or severe behaviours as effectively as formal security checks.

Create magic

The best platforms address all three categories of transaction costs. They also use data to learn and to reduce friction further. Everything works smoothly together without any effort. That's why it feels like magic.

Therefore, don't just focus on one type of transaction costs, but consider the whole value chain. Figure 2.1 below describes how. For example, reduce

FIGURE 2.1   How to create frictionless experience

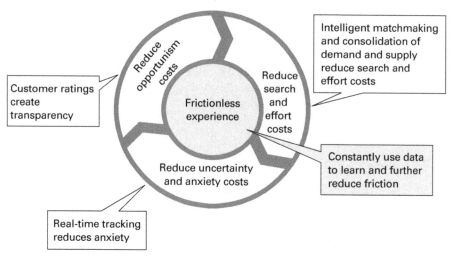

search and effort costs by consolidating demand and supply powered by intelligent matchmaking. Provide real-time tracking to alleviate uncertainty and anxiety costs and address opportunism by customer ratings.

Note also that the same mechanism can lead to a reduction of all of these costs. For example, the five-star rating system is very effective. Feedback ensures a better match for the customer's needs, leading to less search and effort costs. It also increases trust and thus reduces uncertainty and anxiety. Finally, the mere fact that customers and users know feedback is given reduces opportunism.

But, the catch is that you enforce the feedback. It's critical to show that the ratings have a direct impact on the quality of the service. For instance, a badly behaving passenger might not get rides anymore. Or bad reviews for Airbnb leads to fewer rentals. And it goes in the other direction as well. Bad reviews for a traveller renting Airbnb property impact his or her chances of renting any property through Airbnb.

Key takeaways for your organization

By reducing transaction-related friction, you can change the game and create new platforms. If there is high friction for accessing and using current services, this might be an opportunity for you to create a platform.

But they can also prevent your platform from engaging its users. The effort required from potential platform members to find your platform or engage with it might be too high. The uncertainty and anxiety related to their use might make them prefer an alternative solution. The risk of another platform member cheating, stealing or lying might cause potential users to go somewhere else. As you are developing your platform, you need to identify relevant friction in your platform and take decisive action to minimize it.

Search and effort costs

- How do your customers and other members of the platform find the platform and its services? What actions do they need to take to find and engage with the platform?
- Could you consolidate supply and demand by creating a marketplace or generate intelligent matches by recognizing parameters underlying needs and supply?
- How could you minimize the number of decisions platform members need to take to get started to use your platform?
- What unused assets could your platform orchestrate to increase value for its members?
- What technologies could you use to minimize friction in your platform?

Uncertainty and anxiety costs

- What information are different members of your platform always waiting for to make sure things are going as they should be?
- Is there a way for you to provide real-time tracking or other updates for the platform members to reassure them?
- What rich media forms, such as images, animations or sounds, could you share with platform members to make them feel that things are happening as they should be?
- Do people consider your platform reliable and trustworthy? What alternative paths could there be to (further) improve your reputation?

Opportunism-related costs

- In the rare occasions that they behave immorally, how might members of your platform cheat, steal, lie or otherwise exploit the platform or its other members?

- What behaviours could you track and share with other platform members? Is it possible to do it on all sides of the platform?
- How does your platform promote transparency in the market? Could you do more?
- What rules, penalties and safeguards does your platform apply to prevent opportunistic behaviours? Are their benefits higher than the additional friction they create?

CHAPTER THREE

Focus your actions to create fans

All successful platforms started with a narrow focus. It helped them to build a loyal following of fans.

In the previous chapter, we showed you how to remove friction. Platforms emerge from identifying industries and processes which had high friction and removing it. Like Peloton, which disrupted the fitness space industry by making group fitness classes fun and accessible. Once you have selected a process or service where you want to simplify things, you need to choose where to start and how to expand.

When Apple entered the mobile phone market in 2007, it launched only one touchscreen device, the iPhone. Many considered this a mistake as other vendors offered many devices with several form factors and use cases. But, as the smartphone market developed, consumer preferences had changed. Consequently, Apple seized the moment and went against conventional wisdom. Its focused approach with only one single smartphone won the game. Focus is essential when a new business is emerging.

Focus is also essential to create value. Suppose the benefits of the service a platform provides are not clear. In that case, users are unlikely to invite friends or colleagues to use it. On the other hand, a simple and straightforward value proposition encourages them to share and invite others to strengthen network effects. With a clear value proposition, you reduce the emotional risk of sharing. Customers can share their enthusiasm without being embarrassed by sharing an unclear offering.

So, how do you select your focus? How do you choose the next steps after the initial focus? And what creates community? This chapter will guide you through three simple steps to start to build a successful platform:

1 Focused launch – define a focused offering and build engagement from an initial narrow set of customers.
2 Refine and expand – expand customer base and platform scope incrementally.
3 Build an engaged community – create an experience that rewards participants and produces advocates for your service.

Successful platforms start with a focused offering

The path to a successful platform does not start from a broad offering. Instead, building a thriving platform requires, almost paradoxically, patient and relentless focus on a single core product or service. Such attention is needed because you become exciting and relevant to partners only if you have something unique and highly value-adding to give. And the best way to build something unique and highly value-adding is to focus all your efforts on creating that unique thing.

The first Tesla, Model S, didn't seem like a platform. It was a very focused offering, just one car targeted for the luxury segment for environmentally conscious people who wanted a high-end electric vehicle. With its long range, it removed the friction and anxiety about charging the car battery.

Peloton is an interactive fitness platform. It provides high-end bikes costing over US $2,000, which you can use at home to participate in fitness classes with other people. When it launched in 2013, it had a very sharp offering. Peloton sold nicely designed indoor exercise bikes connected to the internet. Furthermore, it offered live and pre-recorded group classes in people's homes. So, anybody can participate in bike-exercise training – and nothing more.

Focus drives up usage and builds devoted fans. There is a temptation to expand your company's offering, especially if your technology and platform are powerful. But the only thing that matters is that your users see enough value. A minimum viable product is not the one you can launch for scale. It is the one that satisfies customers, offering them enough value. Be clear on who your customers are and what they need, focusing on a well-specified customer segment with a narrow offering. You are then more likely to succeed in the launch and build a platform at a later stage.

The most successful platform companies, Amazon, Facebook and Uber, sequenced their platforms' development. They initially focused on getting engagement from a narrowly defined set of customers. These customers were often physically proximate to one another. After the initial focus, they started generating other elements that expanded the business model over time.

Companies that start with a focused approach dedicate most of their development resources on making a single product or service work effectively. And they do it for a clearly defined and narrow customer group. The immediate benefit of this approach is that they make fast progress concerning that single product or service. In contrast, companies that dedicate the same amount of resources on developing multiple products or services spread themselves more thinly and therefore make slower progress per product or service.

Facebook, Uber and other companies did not become platforms accidentally. There is a clear pattern of how they built their platform. In the following, we explain how to create a platform by focusing your actions. Any company, large or small, can execute this.

As an incumbent, the advantage you have is the assets you already have, the customers you already have, but these are also your biggest obstacles. You need to rethink the way you operate to succeed against new competition.

Create your focused offering with these steps

It is easy to say you should focus and drop everything else. However, choosing what to focus on can be a challenge. The following steps will help you find your initial focus and expand over time.

Four steps to create and launch a focused offering:

1 Backtrack from your vision

2 Experiment and explore to find the most effective first step

3 Start from a friendly geographical region or market niche

4 Design your core to be supported by the best existing solutions and technologies

---

1. Backtrack from your vision

You need to start in a focused manner, but not without a great vision. The problem is many wannabe platforms get over-excited about their vision. They dream big and – naturally – want to make the future a reality as soon as possible. They, therefore, implement too many things simultaneously, which stretches them too thin and confuses potential clients and partners.

What you need to do instead is to backtrack from your vision: imagine the future and then create a practical path from your current state to the vision. In this way, you can leverage the inspiring power of the vision without losing focus in actions – you are building something more significant, but one step at a time.

To create an effective path from today's reality to your vision, you should first create several alternative routes. As illustrated in Figure 3.1 below, each route should identify several steps that could take you from the present situation to the vision.

The steps should also be cumulative: the first step provides a foundation for the second step. For Amazon, the first step was to sell books, and the second step was to sell other items. As the first step helped in capability building for e-commerce and made Amazon famous, it contributed to the success of the second step.

As illustrated in the above figure, the alternative paths can differ substantially from one another. You should aim to create very different pathways from the present to your vision. From these alternative paths, you will select the one that creates the highest customer value immediately or removes the most significant pain point in the current process.

The first step should not be too complicated. A rich feature set might confuse customers as you are trying to change the current way of operating.

However, you should not confuse 'complicated' with 'value-adding'. You need the latter while avoiding the former. This is not always easy. Sometimes, you need to add features to pass the threshold for value-adding.

For example, a diagnosis service for dogs offered to vets initially focused on providing only diagnosis and recommendation for the most suitable drugs. However, older veterinarians were not interested in using it. They think they are the ones who know how to diagnose animals (regardless of whether it is true or not). Although young vets were interested in using it, they also might reduce or abandon the use when they develop their skills.

FIGURE 3.1   How to define alternative pathways to vision

The founding team analysed the situation and discussed it with their advisers. Vets enjoy discussing symptoms and often ask for help for diagnosing in closed social media forums. Therefore, the team decided to add this type of feature to the service. Now, there is a reason for vets to use the service to help other vets or just observe what other vets are discussing.

2. Experiment and explore to find the most effective first step

It is excellent if you can start with a vision and then backtrack from it. However, sometimes it is difficult to envision the end state, even if you have several great ideas. In such a situation, you can move forward by experimenting and exploring various paths to learn what works and what doesn't.

Experimenting: If you already have customers, you could start by testing a feature set with them. First, offer a more extensive feature set and then remove some of them to try their value with a limited sample. This process gives you an assessment of the importance of different elements in your offering and helps to decide the launch offer.

You could also test the different paths you created in the backtracking exercise, see what works best, and then select the most promising one.

Experimentation might be resource intensive. Therefore, you need to work in agile mode to ensure fast enough progress – make decisions quickly and reallocate resources flexibly.

Discovering a latent need just outside your current boundary is another technique for established companies to define an initial focus for a platform offering. Many of us have struggled with the Swedish invention, IKEA's self-assembly furniture. IKEA's discovery that their customers need help in assembly when they buy their products is an excellent example of detecting a latent need.

First, IKEA decided to offer these services by themselves. However, it saw a more considerable opportunity. In 2017, IKEA made its first acquisition in its 76-year history. It bought Task Rabbit, a contract labour marketplace. IKEA decided to run TaskRabbit as an independent company.

After discovering the latent need, you move to define the vision and then apply backtracking to determine the first step for your launch. For example, through TaskRabbit, IKEA started furniture assembly with a limited geographical focus in New York City and San Francisco locations (Angulo, 2018).

Another Swedish example of discovering latent need is Spotify. Instead of fighting incumbents, like Apple iTunes, with digital downloads, it focused on an emerging niche, streaming. Its founder Daniel Ek saw that people were ready to pay a small fee or listen to advertising for unlimited music access. Illegal services like Napster had already proven the latent need. Spotify offered the same experience legally.

Interviewing customers, suppliers and other stakeholders is a useful technique to define what would add the most value to your customers and other stakeholders in both the short and long term. Before doing interviews, you should already have a sketch of your target in mind. Ask what your customers value at the moment and how to strengthen it.

1 Interview a select set of trusted customers
   a Ask them to describe their core processes in an open-ended way
   b Seek to understand what are the most value-adding and difficult elements in the process.
2 Model the customer's process in simple diagrams
   a Start by making individual parts of the process on separate slides
   b Once you have created some three–eight slides, move towards building a synthesis.
3 Reflect on how your company is currently helping them in the critical processes. Reflect also where you are not presently helping but potentially could.
4 Consider which step is providing the most value for the customer, from their point of view (many of your actions help, but which one of them helps the most).
5 Imagine a path where you first start with the most value-adding element and then build on top of that.

Consider also conducting three–five interviews with selected suppliers to understand the platform's value from their point of view. It's critical to recognize relevant stakeholders and their likely reaction to the platform via conceptual work and discussions. By conceptual work, we mean that you should in advance try to anticipate how somebody would react to the platform proposition. The goal is to guide them to perceive the platform as beneficial for them.

Document everything carefully. Who are the platform participants, their roles and what value do they get out of the platform? Define the architecture and business model of the platform. Describe also your current state, customers, suppliers, processes and assets you have.

Combine this step with your vision and backtracking from there into the first focused offering.

3. Start from a friendly geographical region or market niche

Decoding the platform winners' recipe shows they don't try to serve and please everybody and all markets. They start from limited geography or from a market niche and expand from there. Experimentation is also more manageable in a smaller market. Companies often fail by scaling too early before they have found the right product. But don't take the early narrow focus as a sign of being satisfied with a small market. On the contrary, focus, in the beginning, allows you to find the right feature set for scaling.

Facebook initially focused on building a static social network within a concentrated physical location of a university campus. In this way, the company could concentrate all its efforts on making the service as good as possible for that narrowly defined customer group. Zuckerberg populated the platform with data he had acquired from the university's housing services. In this way, he made the platform value-adding for every Harvard student. In essence, they could see all their friends' profiles on the platform and a draft profile for themselves. Therefore, they were motivated to improve their own profile, which made the platform more value-adding for their friends.

Uber initially operated only high-end limousine service in a single city. This approach helped it refine its software platform, pricing policies and other practices such that it became an even more reliable and user-friendly service. The company concentrated on a single geographical area. Therefore, its managers were able to gather insights from that area and dedicate their mental effort to understanding the dynamics. This mental effort helped in making the service even better. It increased the customers' commitment to and excitement about the service.

Amazon likewise started with a relatively simple online bookstore, and focused its efforts on doing the bookstore work exceptionally well. It had a comprehensive inventory of books, and you could get any book you wanted from Amazon. In contrast, no other bookstore could hold an equally extensive stock. The recommendation engine (people who bought this book also liked these books) and other features made the service smooth, value-adding and created network effect. Amazon thus became the choice for buying books.

The first phase in the development of these now complex and global platform companies was, in sum, a very focused and local service that worked exceptionally well. The superior quality of the narrow service generated vast excitement among the users of the service. The excitement helped to build a broader reputation for the platform. For example, once Harvard students got excited about Facebook, they started using it even more and also told their friends in other universities about the service. Similarly, people who had a positive experience with Uber or Amazon became more likely to use the service again and tell their friends about it.

CASE STUDY   Peloton: Removing friction from home exercise

The year 2020 was a great one for Peloton. As the Covid-19 pandemic raged on, people wanted to exercise at home. Peloton has more than a million monthly customers, and it has expanded its business with treadmills and yoga, and other exercise classes. It didn't happen by accident, but following the steps outlined in this and the previous chapter: ie removing friction and being focused.

Peloton founders experienced too much friction in trying to get into a spinning class. First, it was hard to find time for fitness classes in your busy schedule. And even if you had time, it was challenging to find a great instructor and a class. And the per-class fee was prohibitive (Huddleston, 2019).

When expanding, platform companies follow their vision. Many think of Peloton as a fitness company. But, according to Peloton's founders, Peloton is a media-technology-retail-logistics company (Huddleston, 2019).

Peloton had a focused offering with sleek-design bikes and live and on-demand cycling classes. Only after this offering became successful did it expand into other types of exercise that today manifest its popularity.

Sometimes you need to make changes to ensure your focused offering is perceived right. First, Peloton charged US $1,200 for the indoor exercise bike. However, due to the relatively low price, customers perceived that the equipment must be poorly built. Thus, they increased the price to over US $2,000, and sales went up. Perception of the bike's quality changed from poor to excellent just because of the price change (Mangalindan, 2019).

Now you might point out that so far we have focused on platforms only for B2C. The question remains how does this impact any other type of traditional business? It's easy to discuss Facebook, Uber and other well-known examples and dismiss them as something that happens somewhere there, outside of other industries.

There are some specifics which aspiring B2B platform providers should consider. A B2B platform's services or products may be critical for business continuity and carry substantial risk for the customer. Therefore, quality and service level must be right from the first transaction as customers have high expectations (Anding, 2019).

Platforms are already making a difference in traditional manufacturing industries. An excellent example is Tetra Pak, which provides spare parts and consumables through a B2B marketplace.

CASE STUDY   Tetra Pak's focused platform launch

Tetra Pak sells manufacturing and packaging facilities for the food and beverage industry. For example, the raw material is processed in manufacturing facilities operated by Tetra Pak's customers and then packaged using packaging facilities and Tetra Pak's packing materials. Tetra Pak works with 5,000 manufacturing plants that produce a combined 190 billion consumer packages around the world (Tetra Pak, 2020).

Tetra Pak founded its own platform in 2019 as a proactive move. Like Amazon, Tetra Pak does not only provide their own spare parts and consumables through the marketplace, but it also offers third-party products. It has 300,000 spare parts and consumables from Tetra Pak and 200,000 products from vetted third-party sellers.

According to Tetra Pak's vice president for parts and consumables, Klara Svedberg, customers expect more convenience, efficiency and transparency (Tetra Pak, 2020). Tetra Pak's marketplace creates a one-stop shop solution, which offers exactly that. So, in this case, Tetra Pak uses the power of platforms and ecosystems for their benefit.

Tetra Pak could have offered a much more extensive selection of services already from the launch. But it decided to focus. For B2B customers, the narrow offering was understandable and thus encouraged companies to start to use it.

As the marketplace needs the suppliers to participate, the obvious question is 'why would they?'. The answer: a marketplace provides a new sales channel. In the case of Tetra Pak, it is global. Suppliers get new sales opportunities.

Tetra Pak operates globally, but they need to provide local solutions. Very often, a specific supplier to Tetra Pak is local. As Tetra Pak is creating a one-stop shop, it is tempting to pack everything from the start. They could be selling spare parts, consumables, adhesives, lubricants, chemicals and services (services include installation or consulting). So they could have imagined a complete, ideal solution and then backtracked from there to the current offering they launched in 2019, offering spare parts and consumables only.

Tetra Pak's marketplace is powered by Mirakl. Mirakl is kind of a modern-day SAP that powers marketplaces. SAP has been extremely successful by creating software to manage enterprise business processes. Time will tell whether Mirakl will be as dominant as SAP. However, it shows that every company does not need to build its own software to create a marketplace. Mirakl provides marketplace functionalities as a service. Of course, you need to define your business model still and possibly develop applications and a user interface to get the marketplace model's full benefits.

To identify a friendly region or niche for your platform, you should consider where you are most likely to succeed. Several factors can influence your chances of success. You can start by considering the following:

- Boundaries of the market: is the market homogeneous enough to be defined as a single market. For example, the US is not a market but has several markets such as New York, Houston and San Francisco.
- Your familiarity with the market: how well do you know the potential customers and their needs, habits and preferences? How well do you know the regulation and other contextual constraints?
- Competition within the market: are there already several other companies targeting the same region or niche?
- Availability of resources: will you hire the needed talent from the region and satisfy the niche?
- Stepping stone: where can you expand from the first region or niche if you are successful?
- Synergy with a current offering: can you leverage your existing capabilities, channels and marketing efforts, or do you need to create everything anew for the region or niche?

4. Design your core to be supported by the best existing solutions and technologies

Creating a focused offering requires that you recognize your service's soul, the one focused offering that makes your product or service stand out from the rest. Often, creating the best possible core requires leveraging several complementary technologies and solutions. Therefore, you should design your core so that it can leverage the existing solutions and technologies as much as possible. Often, this means compromising on the scope of the product to be able to connect the core to a more robust set of technologies that place (temporary) constraints to use cases.

CASE STUDY   Varjo's human-eye resolution VR system

Connie was about to dock the spacecraft to a space station. She glanced at the metres and noticed with satisfaction that she could see the smallest of details on the crew console. She had done the docking numerous times, but this was different. Everything happened in virtual reality powered now by the new Varjo human-eye resolution VR system. Varjo collaborates with the Boeing Starliner programme opening up unprecedented virtual reality training opportunities for a crewed space mission. For the VR training to be effective, astronauts need to read all the displays simultaneously while operating the simulated aircraft with their hands. With earlier VR headsets, reading the terminals in the immersive training environment was only possible when leaning in close to the displays – but then the astronauts couldn't see their hands, making it unsuitable for training (Varjo, 2020).

Varjo is a Finnish start-up that originated from the remnants of Nokia. Its founders Niko, Klaus, Roope and Urho, share a passion for multimedia systems and once worked together in Nokia. Its current CEO, Timo Toikkanen, sat on the executive board of Nokia and was responsible for Nokia's incredibly successful basic phone business.

Varjo revolutionizes professional virtual reality by bringing every detail, texture, contour and colour into focus – even for users who wear glasses or contact lenses. Furthermore, the system can combine virtual with outside reality, creating a mixed-reality environment.

Mike Leach, solution portfolio lead at Lenovo, said 'many existing VR offerings in the market today are enterprise versions of a consumer-designed product' (2020). In contrast, instead of seeking to reach the mass market in every potential VR/AR segment, Varjo focused on engineers working on desktops designing motors and other systems. Concentrating on the market niche helped Varjo make faster progress in product development. And it gained traction with customers like Boeing and Volvo as well as partners like Lenovo. Users can purchase 'Certified for Varjo' Lenovo workstations along with any device available in Varjo's portfolio via Lenovo's distribution channels.

But the priorities are more apparent when it comes to product features. Varjo is not making its own graphic processors for VR but uses the existing best processors from the marketplace. As graphics technology develops with giant leaps, the latest commercial processors enable the best possible user experience.

This approach was possible due to Varjo's focus on designer-engineers and other limited mobility use cases. As Varjo's glasses do not need such high mobility, an optical cord can connect them to a computer. Hence, the graphic processor needs not to be inside the headset but on a regular computer. The best components can be used for processing the visual images, and only the screen technology needs to be in the headset. This architecture also enables easy software updates.

Putting graphics processing into the headset would have slowed down the development cycle significantly. Thus, Varjo made a tough decision to provide the best VR experience, easy software, and hardware updates with limited mobility. However, it selected an optical cord, also the best off-the-shelf solution, instead of traditional copper wire. Optical cables enable a more extended, lighter and less disturbing connection between the central and VR glasses.

And in the future, low latency 5G wireless technology can replace the optical cord enabling full mobility. Suddenly, the architecture with some compromises turns into state of the art, extending Varjo's lead.

Successful start-ups in the nascent financial-technology market are focusing on developing some of their core elements. And they are borrowing other elements from their peers. For example, in a recent study by Harvard and Stanford professors (McDonald and Eisenhardt, 2019), one of the most successful start-ups, Zeus (anonymized), copied its rival's user interface and used the same data-analytics provider as another rival. The company leaders made this choice because they wanted to dedicate all their efforts to developing the unique and most value-adding elements of their service. Rather than reinvent elements that other companies had already invented.

Focusing on a single product or service and, often, also on a subset of unique features in that product or service enables the use of the best available components from the marketplace. Companies that focus do not seek to create everything by themselves. Still, they scan the marketplace and use the available products and services as components in their own product and service. In this way, they ensure that their offering is on the cutting edge of development.

For your platform, what could be the best available technologies and solutions that could support the core of your service or product? What prevents you from using them? Could you reduce these constraints by leaving out a subset of users or use cases? In other words, could you improve your product or service by focusing more in a way that would enable you to leverage better external solutions and technologies?

Continuous refinement and incremental expansion

After starting with a focused offering, successful platform companies continuously refine their offering and expand with incremental steps. They build on the momentum created by their initial, focused offering while adding new features and elements that attract more customers or fans.

CASE STUDY   Getting better mile by mile – Tesla

In December 2019, some Tesla Model 3 owners saw a software upgrade option: 'Improve your 0-60 mph acceleration from 4.4 seconds to 3.9 seconds with an over-the-air update'. The price for 0.5 seconds faster acceleration was US $2,000.

The upgrade was just one example of how Tesla updates software over the air, continually improving the car's features and functionality. Each Tesla software update makes your car feel like new. Most of the upgrades are free; they just appear, and suddenly, for example, you got a 5 per cent improvement in the range of the car.

Other upgrades include driving visualization, which can display stoplights, stop signs and road markings. Probably in the future, Tesla can also automatically react to these signs. We will cover more on the learning loop and how Tesla autopilot learns in the next chapter.

As Tesla owns the software platform, it controls the experience. Therefore, it can expand the platform's scope incrementally, unlike other car vendors operating like product companies.

Tesla follows the suit of successful platform companies. Having created a reputation by zooming to a specific offering, the platform companies started incrementally expanding to other areas to broaden their scope.

You can even select if you want your software upgrades immediately as soon they become available or a bit later once early adopters have used them for a while. So you can decide to be the one who gets to try new things first. Or you can wait until others have tested the new software and sorted out possible teething problems.

Tesla also applied an incremental expansion strategy to its fleet. Following its successful focused entry into the market, Tesla introduced the sport utility vehicle, Tesla X, expanding the customer base. Mass market, and with a lower price point, Tesla Model 3 was launched next. It soon became one of the bestselling car models among all brands in many markets. Tesla Y, a crossover, was introduced to the market in 2020, and a much-discussed Cybertruck is expected to be available in 2021. So what started as a one-model luxury car company is now offering a full fleet of cars. And we can expect it will expand to new models going forward. Each of these further incremental steps is building momentum for the company.

Refine and expand your platform with these steps

You should continuously refine and incrementally expand your offering. Continuous refinement and expansion requires patient and systematic efforts over time. You should not hurry but calmly reflect and observe to take practical actions. In this way, you can move fast without rushing. The following steps will help you.

Four steps to refine and expand your platform:

1 Observe and experiment to refine each element of your platform

2 Create new features and services

3 Enter new locations

4 Redo backtracking

1. Observe and experiment to refine each element of your platform

To refine your focused offering, you should be relentless and data driven. See what works and what does not. Change what does not work and keep what does. In this way, you build an ever-stronger commitment and a more robust foundation for adding new features and services. Two critical methods for refining your platform are observations and A/B-testing (comparing two versions to see which one performs better).

Observe behaviour. During each step, the platform companies actively use data analytics to improve the quality of the service continuously. For example, when you log into Facebook, the company records your every move. How long you read each post you see, where you place the mouse, what you click on, how fast you return and so on. The company analyses what content and which mode of presenting the content you like the most from this data. Hence, the next time you are likely to see more content you want and less content you dislike. Based on the analytics, Facebook can also define customer segmentation and decide the best ones to select for expansion.

Amazon is optimizing its website and associated user experience regularly to improve customer engagement. The recommendation engine can keep a customer browsing the Amazon site for a longer period of time. In addition, various details related to the website look and navigation influence how long customers remain on the site, and Amazon is continually improving these features.

Another big part of Amazon's approach to keeping customers engaged is direct email contact. Rather than waiting for the customers to return to the site, Amazon sends recommendation emails that occasionally bring the customer back.

Uber has hired a team of behavioural scientists to maximize the company's understanding of customer behaviours. Uber Labs consists of psychologists, marketing professionals and cognitive scientists. They analyse how customers react to Uber's current and potential services and features. Their insights provide essential information for refinement and expansion decisions (Kamat and Hogan, 2019).

Run A/B tests to experiment. In addition to observing your behaviour, Facebook is continuously running A/B testing, as is Amazon. One portion of the users gets to view one version of a particular aspect of the service, while another gets to see another. The companies then track how the users behave and select the version that produces better results for continued use.

Uber has a unique experimentation platform, XP, for A/B and other tests. It enables Uber to launch, debug, measure and monitor the effects of new ideas, product features, marketing campaigns, promotions and even machine learning models (Anirban *et al*, 2020).

Peloton is also continually running A/B tests for new or improved features. For example, during a workout, riders can cheer each other on with high fives. If you ride in a large group, it's hard to find the person who gave the high five on the leaderboard. So you cannot follow them back.

Peloton was A/B testing a feature where you can now click on members who give you high fives. Thus, you can send them a high five, see their current ranking or open their profile to send them a follow request (L, 2020). Based on these types of A/B tests, it either adds features to all users, modifies or removes them.

How would you do this on your platform? You should start with a commitment to continuous improvement. After that, reflect which aspects of customer behaviour are the most important to observe and which new features could be tested.

2. Create new features and services

After the launch and getting significant traction it's time to start expanding the offering. New features and services broaden the appeal of your platform. Gradually, you are tapping into new user segments and scaling your platform. Furthermore, new features will also drive higher engagement. But remember to tie this step to the previous one. Observe and measure the success of new features and services.

There are several dimensions one can consider. What customer segments? What geographies? What features to add? How to develop to become a one-stop shop?

The expansions can be natural extensions of the initial offering. Peloton started with the training bike and spinning classes. For them, it was natural to expand into treadmills. In this way, it provided variety in the training. It also attracted runners in addition to cyclists. The next step was an increase in the types of exercises: high-intensity interval training, barre, yoga, boot-camp and meditation (Huddleston, 2019). Peloton also expanded its digital distribution channels. Its app is now available through Roku TV, Amazon Fire TV, Apple TV and Android TV. Additionally, Peloton is expanding into other original content types by increasing its music library and collaborating with famous artists (Thomas, 2020).

Facebook used to be a relatively static platform – users would simply create their profiles and fill them with some information, such as favourite quotes and books and some photos. However, many users did not return to Facebook very often to look at their friends' static profiles; ie they were not very engaged with the service.

To make Facebook more engaging, the company introduced the newsfeed. Users could now see in a single feed what was happening in their network. The feed showed if someone had uploaded new photos or updated their status. In this way, whenever a user opened Facebook, they could immediately see various recent developments. The updates made the service more rewarding and also generated some fear of missing out (FOMO). Therefore, users returned to the site more often. This is what we call *reason-to-go-back* expansion.

Uber leveraged its initial momentum and expanded to regular cars in select cities. Initially, the service was constrained to limousines, but the founders realized that there was a pool of people owning any type of vehicle to drive passengers. They thus introduced Uber X, which benefitted from the Uber brand, but was targeted to a broader customer group. As the limousine service had already build legitimacy and excitement, the new service did not come out of the blue for ride seekers. Still, they could have a rough understanding of the service and were willing to experiment. This strategy is called *price tiers*.

Amazon's most significant expansion steps were product categories. Once the book business was becoming ever smoother, the company realized that it could also sell other products via the platform. Hence, it added toys, electronics and other relatively easy products to sell via online channels. For instance, products that could be shipped as standard mail packages (rather than fresh or frozen food, for example) or did not need much fitting (eg clothes). In this way, Amazon expanded its product scope but did not overly complicate its processes or take unbearable service quality-related risks.

IKEA leveraged its TaskRabbit platform to bundle same-day delivery and assembly for IKEA products. TaskRabbit is also expanding into interior design and looking at services such as furniture repair to give IKEA an edge.

New data sources can be essential drivers for new products and services. For example, according to IKEA management, TaskRabbit's customer data could help IKEA develop new ideas for furniture (Rinstrom and Fares, 2019).

How do you invent and build new features and services for your platform? You can get started by considering the same criteria you used to select the initial focus, as described above. Furthermore, you can also leverage several creativity-boosting techniques we describe in Chapter 6, 'Create the unexpected'.

3. Enter new locations

Once you start thriving in a single location, you should build on the momentum and enter new places. For Facebook, the natural next step after conquering Harvard was to expand to other Ivy League universities. The students in these universities shared a similar elite identity, and many of them also knew one another. Hence, a service that allowed a Stanford student to connect with his fellow Stanford students and his friends at Harvard immediately generated value for them. Again, the cycle of positive excitement was reinforced. This is what we call *focused on geographical expansion*.

Subsequently, Facebook benefitted from this excitement and continued expanding its scope: it first opened up to all US universities and, ultimately, after several steps, to all the people in the world. But it did not start with all the people in the world because such an approach would not have generated the initial excitement that resulted from the geographically contained initial focus.

Peloton has followed the bike's inquiries as an indicator of the demand for its service (Peloton, 2019). After launching in major cities in the US, Peloton focused its international expansion first to Canada and the UK. Both are sizeable English-speaking gym markets. In addition to its online direct-to-consumer sales, it opened multiple owned retail locations, similar to Tesla. These locations will provide an opportunity for new customers to experience Peloton physically.

In the UK, Peloton launched a London-based studio and added British instructors. Next, Peloton launched in Germany, where over 10 million people belong to a gym (Peloton, 2019). But, there was no need to build one more studio. German instructors can teach from the London studio, and Peloton streams the classes to Germany. Also, to expand access to its current content, Peloton provided German subtitles for hundreds of English-language classes.

Although its partner TaskRabbit had a larger footprint, IKEA had a very deliberate geographical expansion of its furniture assembly service. It needs to make sure its service personnel is ready and the specific pricing is in place. It also needs to ensure there are enough qualified taskers in place.

Since IKEA's acquisition in 2017, TaskRabbit has expanded to all 48 US cities with IKEA stores and launched in Canada (Rinstrom and Fares, 2019). In the UK, it has moved beyond London to several new cities.

When evaluating which region your platform should enter next, you can use the same criteria you used to select the initial focus described above. You should also remember the next region need not be a country, but it can be, for example, a particular city or community.

4. Redo backtracking

After you have executed one step in your path toward your vision, you need to select the next step. For this, you apply the backtracking technique again by evaluating alternative paths towards your ultimate vision. You should also check if this modifies the vision and whether the paths are still the same, or you should also modify them. Then again, you select the pathway which adds the highest customer value or removes the highest pain point in the process.

Engaged communities multiply platform value

Besides developing and expanding their offering, successful platforms actively engage the platform stakeholders into a community. Engaged communities are more than a pool of users and suppliers – they are individuals who are excited about the platform's product or service and want to share their excitement with others: they are fans. They offer improvement suggestions, help one another in problem solving, and even lobby for more beneficial legislation and infrastructure.

In short, members of an engaged community love the product or service and want to make it even more successful. Their energy helps the platform improve and grow. By connecting on multiple levels, they create an engaged community. Thus, the community strengthens the network effect and creates value for participants and the platform.

To create an engaged community, you should make an experience that rewards participants and creates advocates for your service. Creating an experience is not a technical thing, but the most critical thing is empathy creation with the customer. You need to understand your customers empathetically and see their point of view. Only then can you create a meaningful offering that they enthusiastically embrace. Creating fans and engagement is not a trick but is a much deeper thought process.

Traditional sales and marketing starts from the notion that you create a funnel and move people through it. First, develop prospects, then convert them into sales.

When creating a platform, you should think differently. You focus on people who are ready for the change and become fans and ambassadors from the start – like Tesla and Peloton.

We call it *engagement circle* – it's like dropping a stone into water. The first waves are the highest, and then they will wane, but the bigger the splash at the beginning, the larger the impact. With the engagement circle, you focus on the middle, the most enthusiastic customers, to make them advocates.

Customer engagement means interaction with your platform, ie the service and experience you are offering. A new customer might come and log in but not continue to interact. That's low engagement. Another customer has used the service several times and has referred several friends or colleagues who have also logged in. That's high engagement and high value.

Amazon has a special consumer engagement team. It's a group of researchers, designers and technology professionals who work across Amazon. They invent, build and manage the features that give Amazon customers the feeling that Amazon knows them. Of course, data serves as a cornerstone for the whole process, as we discuss in the next chapter.

But you should not limit customer engagement just to the use of your service. Equally important is to understand your customers' social media interactions. These include liking, sharing and commenting on content, participation in community events and meet-ups and writing reviews. For example, Amazon's consumer engagement team also owns social sharing systems, including gamification and moderation.

Formally, a broader definition of customer engagement is customers' willingness to spend their time on the company for mutual benefit, often through brand advocacy or other involvement (Astute Solutions, 2019).

Build an engaged community with these steps

To build an engaged community, you should first understand what makes your platform's customers and other stakeholders engaged. After that, take actions to increase engagement, expand the community, and intensify the community's interaction. You should follow these four steps:

Four steps to build an engaged community for your platform:

1 Measure engagement continuously
2 Prioritize emotions in experience design
3 Nudge and enable friction-free referrals
4 Enable community communication and shared identification

1. Measure engagement continuously

To understand your customer engagement, you should set goals and measure your outcomes. Metrics for customer engagement are lifetime value (LTV, the total amount of money a customer is expected to spend in your business during their lifetime), frequency of use, churn and many other traditional marketing metrics. But you should also measure customer referrals, advocacy on social media, reviews and participation in community events.

According to the Gallup (2014) study of B2B customers, fully engaged customers deliver a 23 per cent premium over average customers in the share of wallet, profitability, revenue and relationship growth. Due to network effects, platforms amplify customer engagement. High engagement will multiply across the ecosystem.

And remember, retaining old customers is cheaper than the acquisition of new customers. And if you can make your old customers acquire new ones, you are better off in the long run.

Often, leaders focus only on growth and metrics for it. However, especially in the beginning, focusing on retention is essential. You want to get people back to service. It's too expensive if you always need to acquire new customers.

For example, Wolt, a Finnish start-up founded in 2014, delivers food and other items to customers in several European countries. In 2015, it almost went bankrupt. During its crisis, Ilkka Paananen, founder of Supercell and an investor at Wolt, reviewed its numbers and metrics. He had learned from the games business that retention is the most important metric for a game. Do people want to return? Is the game important or not? (Raeste, 2020).

From the metrics Wolt CEO Miki Kuusi sent to Paananen, he saw that about half of the people who tried Wolt stayed as customers, which was true month after month. There was a foundation on which one could build – like in the best games. After this, Wolt closed the next investment round swiftly. In 2020, Wolt operated in 23 countries, offered food from 22,450 restaurants, and had 44,000 food couriers (Raeste, 2020).

For your platform, what are the critical customer actions that you might want to follow? How could you measure them?

2. Prioritize emotions in experience design

Emotions are stronger than logic. It's not just the functionality you need to think about. If your customers are emotionally vested in your service, they will likely be highly engaged and become advocates.

Being clear on your purpose will also help companies to create ambassadors. Brands that have a clear purpose create engagement.

You need to design the whole experience to make it unique for your customers. It's not a single element but the entire experience that differentiates the platform from the competition. And if your customers form communities and connect with other customers, this creates genuine engagement and builds real fans and ambassadors.

Tesla is not a car company but has a higher-order purpose of making electric cars accessible and saving the environment. But its offering goes beyond the vehicle. For example, Tesla showrooms are part of the experience (Davis, 2014). Tesla decided to sell direct to consumers and created their own showroom experience. Showrooms are located in malls and drive awareness of Tesla. In the age of social media, everybody who is passing by the exhibition room is a potential advocate as they post pictures and comments on Tesla to social media. Part of Tesla's appeal is also its expansion to home energy systems. It executes its purpose by expanding its business to other areas. We will discuss this further in Chapter 6.

For Peloton, it is not only the bike and service that creates the whole experience but also Peloton's instructors, who are part of the secret sauce (Huddleston, 2019). The cult-like status of Peloton instructors is one of Peloton's most significant advantages over competitors. The instructors' job is to inspire and lead the Peloton community. Robin Arzón is one of the most popular instructors, with 655,000 Instagram followers at the end of 2020.

3. Nudge and enable friction-free referrals

Referrals are an age-old way of attracting clients and generating new business. They are also one of the most common tools to expand and grow your service in the digital era. Thus, make them friction-free and straightforward.

And remember to ask for referrals. A simple nudge after a review or other action goes a long way to activate users of your platform to share a referral. As referrals are often impulsive, spur-of-the-moment actions, creating nudges to trigger such behaviour is essential.

Provide tools to create engagement from your customer base. Creating a simple way to invite friends into service is one way of doing this. And when a user sends an invite, you give a reward: like a free ride in Uber. In this way, you make fans market your service. And fans like when you reward them for loyalty. Just remember that referral mechanism through email or social network needs to feel natural and be straightforward to work.

To create high engagement, understand what your customers value. Some people like a cash reward, some free credits for using the product, some upgrades on their subscription plan, some exclusive features and some VIP experiences. It's hard to know in advance without thorough research and experimentation.

Referrals are also useful in the B2B context. Yammer has become (one of the) most successful social networking services for enterprises. Organization members can use it for informal and private communication at work. Its expansion strategy partly explains Yammer's success: rather than relying solely on formal contracts with companies, Yammer allows individuals with a company email address to create an account. Once a single member of a company has made a Yammer account, they can invite their friends from the same company, who again invite more friends. Thus, Yammer spreads inside the company through peer referrals. Additionally, Yammer has enabled communication between partners, customers, vendors and suppliers, and also, these communications can start with referrals that expand Yammer's reach (Pietruszynski, nd).

Dropbox is a cloud storage platform for file sharing and collaboration. It has a referral programme that rewards users with free storage for friend invites. If you have a Dropbox Basic account, you'll earn 500 MB of space for each friend you refer to Dropbox. And if you have a Dropbox Plus or Professional version, you'll make 1 GB of space for each friend you refer to Dropbox; ie you upgrade your plan to a higher-tier service, and you receive a higher referral reward.

What might be natural points for your platform customers and other stakeholders for making referrals? How could you make referring as easy as possible? How could you reward people for making referrals? How could you nudge them to take action?

4. Enable community communication and shared identification

Without interaction, there is no community. When people interact, a community emerges. You should therefore ensure the members of your platform are not only excited but can also interact.

Active interaction between people creates further excitement, as they can share stories and help one another. Seeing others being excited amplifies their emotional energy. Furthermore, the more they interact, the more they start identifying with one another and the community – people start thinking and feeling that they belong together. The product or service becomes part of who they are. The result is more loyalty, more pro-community actions and even more excitement and engagement.

A community can be an inherent feature of a platform itself, or it could exist in social media. Online communities can also lead to offline communities like meet-ups.

Communities can form even without a company's participation, but the brand often facilitates them. Many companies hire community managers whose task is to increase the community's interaction by providing content and being a discussion opener.

Peloton online communities are full of life and energy. People motivate each other to do even better. They buzz about instructors and share fitness tips (Griffith, 2019). Customers also make many new friends through Peloton, and they travel for meet-ups.

Let the community do the talking for you. This one is not easy as we are so used to push marketing. We are building audiences, not communities. But communities are stronger and create sincere devotion. When developing a community, you should enable your customers to connect, but you cannot control it. If you try to steer the conversation too much, it will backfire.

Tesla customers have built communities that are very strong and engaged. Each country has its local Facebook community, whilst Model 3 has its own. Because Tesla has a higher-order purpose than just making cars, it creates engagement. The fans and ambassadors want to participate. And this is what amplifies the network effect. Not only does every mile I drive make the car better, as it learns (like we will learn in the chapter on learning loops), but every new fan makes the experience better for everybody else as they contribute to the community.

Brands can drive and enable discussion by providing hooks. Tesla's discussion hooks include its autopilot, whether you should keep your hands on the wheel or whether you should pay US $2,000 for half a second acceleration boosts. People discussed these points endlessly in the Tesla Facebook groups and other social media networks.

If you post a question on your problems with Tesla to its Facebook community, you will get an answer immediately and not only one but many. And comments are building on each other. The fans handle customer service.

It's also interesting that even if the manufacturer has faults and makes mistakes, fans forgive them. They discuss errors and issues, but strangely, the brand's mistakes create deeper engagement.

BUILDING B2B COMMUNITIES

Now you might think that communities, fans and ambassadors are only for star companies like Tesla or Peloton. However, any brand, including B2B brands, can benefit from platform leaders' lessons when it comes to creating fans. You just need to provide the opportunity for your customers to engage.

When you start to build a B2B community, aim to understand your audience and their needs by interviewing your customers.

Most professionals like to talk to other professionals. Well-built closed communities can provide peer-to-peer support. Communities provide a place to discuss and engage. A well-crafted community can boost your platform. For example, for a B2B marketplace focused on transactions between buyers and sellers, a B2B community can provide a free forum to discuss or share ideas and interests, solve problems, find business partners and ask for a piece of advice. Community builds engagement and a deeper relationship with your platform.

A community can be closed or open. What works best depends on your business targets. A health company set up a chat service where doctors answer questions and diagnose patients. Doctors operated from remote places, which many doctors liked as it provided an opportunity to work from their homes. The company noticed that online doctors needed support when diagnosing patients. Therefore, the company provided a chat service between doctors who were on duty. Doctors were able to get peer support for the problems they encountered, improving their quality and engagement, and satisfaction.

To get started, you should consider how to enable and facilitate communication among your platform stakeholders. What kinds of interactions would be both emotionally exciting and practically valuable for your community stakeholders? Would it be natural to integrate a communication tool within your platform, or should you create a community through social media networks? What kinds of community events could you organize, both online and offline?

Key takeaways for your organization

As you plan to launch your platform, remember the focus. Being everything to everybody won't cut it. You need to make choices and focus. Focus drives up usage and creates fans who want to come back again and again. And if you manage to build an engaged community out of these fans, it will multiply your platform value.

Create a focused offering

- What is the core service or product your platform is currently offering? Is it clear and focused enough?
- What is the ultimate vision of your platform? What alternative paths do you have toward the vision?
- How could you experiment with which paths generate high value fastest and with a reasonable effort? Which region or niche should you choose first?
- What pre-existing technologies and solutions could you use to support your platform's core to maximize value creation for your primary target segment?

Refine and expand your platform

- What data could you use to improve your platform continuously?
- How could you create new features and services?
- How have you chosen which new locations to enter? What else should you consider?
- Once you have taken your next steps, what new paths toward your ultimate vision might open up?

Build an engaged community

- How do you measure customer and stakeholder engagement with your platform? What else could you measure?
- How might you improve your platform users' emotional experience with the platform?
- How could you nudge and enable your platform members to invite new participants to the platform?
- How could you enable communication between platform stakeholders?

CHAPTER FOUR

Create a learning loop

Intelligent platforms have an AI-powered learning loop. It enables them to improve their value creation and efficiency in new domains rapidly. Once they have entered the industry, they 'run' faster than the incumbents or other entrants and quickly provide more value than others.

For example, Tesla's fleet of over 500,000 vehicles collects data through cameras, radar and other sensors, while people drive their cars. Tesla uses this data to train and improve its AI algorithms. Gradually, Tesla is building a full self-driving capability. And as no other or very few have access to a corresponding amount of data, Tesla is very likely to learn faster than others. Thus, it attracts more customers and makes it even more difficult for its competitors to do the same.

Platform winners collect data on their users and extract learnings all the time. Every improvement attracts more users from whom they can learn more, accelerating the value resulting from network effects.

To win this ever-accelerating race, tap into the power of AI and create a learning loop. It enables you to improve your service in essential areas continuously.

The use of your products and services generates data that you can feed into AI. That helps you make better predictions and insights, allowing you to develop better products and services. And as you become more competitive and attract more customers, you get more data, boosting your service. Learning loops are the key to this virtuous circle.

In this chapter, you will learn how to build a competitive advantage with a learning loop and use data to train AI. Furthermore, we will explain why your employees are a valuable asset to develop AI through human-in-the-loop learning. We will describe three essential elements for building a learning loop:

- Start from business goals.
- Produce relevant data.
- Maximize continuous learning.

We will use the examples of Tesla, Uber and Orica (an explosives provider) to illustrate the process of building a learning loop through each step.

Learning loops strengthen your competitive advantage

When we use Google, it learns from every search and adjusts its AI algorithms and models. Accordingly, the next search is a bit better for everybody. And as every user contributes to the learning loop, Google's lead in search extends further. It has become almost impossible for others to catch up regardless of how good their algorithms are. The one who started earlier will have the advantage forever unless the search paradigm changes.

A learning loop is a virtuous circle where a platform's use creates new data, which improves the platform and its services. And this strengthens your competitive advantage.

CASE STUDY   Tesla's learning loop

Tero was entering the highway with his Tesla 3 on a busy morning. The FSD (Full Self Drive) mode was on, but somehow merging with the traffic wasn't that smooth, and he needed to take control. Two weeks later, the same situation and everything went smoothly. What happened?

Tesla is a learning platform. It collects data through cameras, radar and other sensors. Tesla uses this data to train and improve its AI algorithms.

The next version of the lane change assist is a bit better than earlier versions. Merging into highway traffic from a ramp becomes even smoother, also for Tero. Gradually, Tesla is building a full self-driving capability.

Tesla's architecture allows it to update its cars over the air; new software is delivered wirelessly over Wi-Fi. Every car's self-driving capabilities become better by using data collected by other vehicles. This process contrasts with many other car manufacturers, which don't collect data and update their cars over the air. Tesla's architecture is a platform that allows constant evolution and the use of data.

Tesla's capability to collect data, train AI continuously with new data and update their software with a better version is its learning loop. Thus, the learning loop improves its competitive advantage every day.

In digital companies, a learning loop is easy to build. For example, learning loops target ads and predict what we would like to purchase. With the Internet of Things (IoT) and sensors collecting data from the physical world, building a learning loop has become possible for companies with physical assets. For example, AI can determine parameters for a process in a production facility. Once the facility has executed the process, it compares the outcome to the ideal target state. Consequently, the system adjusts algorithms based on deviations.

Human experts can be the company's most significant asset when creating a learning loop. For example, traditional visual quality control algorithms inspect product flaws in a factory but do not learn from new data. They are programmed once with predetermined rules for defects. But when an expert checks an AI-detected fault, he or she can determine if the flaw is significant or not. The human operator feeds this information back to the system, making it better. The process of a human giving feedback to the system is what constitutes a human-in-the-loop model.

You start the development of a learning loop by defining a business objective. Then you need to understand what data is available to train the AI against the business objective. Next, focus on how you prepare the data to be useful for AI model training. And once you have deployed the AI, it makes decisions, predicts outcomes and creates insights from new data. And based on these, it improves the AI model, further completing the learning loop. Every loop strengthens your competitive advantage.

Effective AI use starts from business goals

People hype AI. Many AI solutions in use today do not add significant value for the companies using them. This is because they have rushed to implement AI pilots and showcases without proper connection to business targets. But for some companies, AI has made all the difference. These companies are using AI smartly in a way that directly contributes to business development and performance.

The challenge for smart use of AI is that you can use various AI tools for multiple purposes. Only a subset of the combinations of tools and purposes are value-adding. However, in the hype, one quickly gets excited and starts acting before thinking.

For intelligent platforms, AI cuts through all operations. For example, a private health care centre might start using AI for various reasons: to improve the efficiency of its administrative procedures, the quality of the patient care, the accuracy of medical diagnosis or price elasticity to maximize profit. Each of these business objectives would require different data. And thus, they have various implications for building the learning loop.

Suppose the objective is to improve the accuracy of medical diagnosis. In this case, the company should build an AI solution that supports doctors in diagnosis. This solution should use various patient-related data, such as demography, specific tests and scientific knowledge about correlations between patient-related attributes and medical conditions. In contrast, if the goal is to maximize profit, the AI system would need more data on factors that predict the patient's willingness to pay. These might include some demographic characteristics but weighted differently, emphasizing different factors. For example, their home address is used as a proxy for wealth.

Ultimately, the goal might be to maximize multiple aspects of the business. Still, it is often more feasible to start with one clear objective because it helps define what data is necessary to collect. Having multiple goals can spread the company's resources too thin and undermine quality. Remember how focus creates fans from the previous chapter.

Two companies could have the same business objective on a superficial level but have a very different strategy for developing AI and their learning loop. For example, self-driving cars' training requires data from videos of millions of miles from different road situations. AI models use the data to learn various types of actions. These include accelerating and slowing down, changing lanes, merging into traffic from a highway ramp or braking when an obstacle appears in front of the car.

Waymo and Tesla approach this business objective in very different ways. Rather than making a perfect system from the start, Tesla decided to apply the learning loop approach. It trained a simple autopilot system to start. By collecting data from the fleet of cars, Tesla is continually improving it. Ultimately it targets a fully self-driving vehicle without the need for a driver.

Waymo, on the other hand, decided to target a more autonomous self-driving car to start with (Hawkins, 2020). Waymo's target is to launch a vehicle that can operate without a driver in limited conditions and routes.

Thus, its AI needs much more comprehensive training than Tesla's initially simple system. Waymo is relying on computer simulations and partners to teach its AI (O'Kane, 2018). As you can see, the company's strategy impacts how you define business goals and what is your data and AI approach.

Not having a clear business goal destroys value and wastes resources. Some companies have become excited about the idea that 'data is the new oil'. Therefore, they collect all the data they can access. However, without a clear picture of how they will use it, they will likely pile up lots of unnecessary data with high cost. Consequently, they fail to conduct focused data collection to solve the matters that truly make a difference to their business.

Develop your business goals for AI with these steps

Follow the steps outlined below to develop your business goals for AI use.

Four steps for developing business goals for AI use:

1 Create a vision of how learning will transform your company

2 Understand what AI can and cannot do

3 Identify key processes as a starting point

4 Create a learning loop for your business goals

---

1. Create a vision of how learning will transform your company

Don't rush to implement AI for the first process that comes to your mind. Start with a vision of how AI will transform your company. Think about how you can create more value for your customers. Do you have valuable expertise that could be scaled by teaching it to AI?

Orica is a more-than-100-year-old Australian company and the world's largest provider of commercial explosives and blasting systems to the mining, quarrying, oil and gas, and construction markets. For AI, Orica's business objective was to improve blasting outcomes for its customers. It realized its engineers were advising customers on implementing blasts. They had valuable knowledge that they could teach to AI (Sherer and Cleghorn, 2018).

Orica started with a tight focus to provide insights and advice to improve blast performance with its AI system, BlastIQ. But, Orica's vision seems to be much larger. The more its customers use its service, the more data it collects, and the better its AI becomes (Sherer and Cleghorn, 2018). This learning loop transforms the company from a manufacturer to an intelligent platform.

2. Understand what AI can and cannot do

AI use cases are numerous. AI can predict energy consumption, translate languages, correct writing mistakes, spot faults in a manufacturing line, analyse investment reports, anticipate traffic delays, recommend the best videos for you and the list goes on.

AI seems to be the solution to everything. Clearly, this is not the case, and AI still has severe limitations. Today's AI is so-called narrow AI. It can perform tasks that are well defined.

The limitations arise from the way AI is trained. AI is excellent in the task you teach it. It learns from historical data. Thus the available data limits the learning capability. Secondly, AI cannot move beyond the original use case very easily.

For example, Finnair and Silo AI built an AI system to predict flight delays. The project's target was to improve air traffic situational awareness for the operations control centre (Silo AI, 2019a). First, the team thought that AI could manage airport congestion all by itself. Although AI shines in predicting delays, it struggles to decide what to do about them. That's where humans outshine AI, and the best end-result is human–machine collaboration.

A severe limitation of AI is that it does not understand causality (cause and effect) beyond rudimentary cases (Bergstein, 2020). AI can be hard to explain. If it is a black box, the users might not use it as they don't trust it.

AI is as good as the data used for teaching it. Data might be biased, resulting in biases in the AI system trained with it. Thus, you should always understand how AI was developed. There are also specific techniques to detect and remove bias from the data.

But remember that AI's capabilities develop fast. What was not possible yesterday might be possible today. So, you need to revisit your decisions from time to time.

3. Identify key processes as a starting point

You have developed your vision and understand what AI can do. Now it's time to define a more explicit business goal and identify the key processes you will begin to put in place to meet that goal.

For example, Uber's key business objective is to direct drivers to match demand to make sure customers get rides when they need them. Therefore, Uber predicts demand and supply to match demand for rides with a proper supply of cars. Predicting demand based on various variables and past patterns is a problem where AI can help.

Uber is also running another real-time process, surge pricing, to optimize the system's overall performance. Sometimes, there is a higher demand than predicted, and Uber cannot deliver enough drivers for a given area. Then Uber increases its prices, attracting more drivers to meet the unexpectedly high demand. Again, this is a clear enough problem that AI can solve.

Keep in mind your competitive advantage – will making the process more intelligent help you to compete better? Is the improvement enough to merit the investment and changes in the processes?

4. Create a learning loop for your business goals

As you have now identified your business objective, you train AI and develop the learning loop. However, don't stop there. Come back to your vision and think about how to define new business goals based on your learning. Consider what new areas you could expand in with a learning loop? What new options do you have that may add unique value to your customers?

And also, think about how you can move to entirely new industries and create new services, as we will describe more in detail in Chapter 6, 'Create the unexpected'.

Learning without data is fantasy

Data is the raw material for AI. Therefore, companies need to understand what data they need to train an AI system, what data they already have and what data needs to be acquired.

As we have explained earlier, Uber predicts demand for rides with AI. It trains AI with data from historical demand patterns, weather, events and many other factors. Uber's AI uses data about global news events, weather, historical pricing, holidays, traffic conditions and the predicted demand for its dynamic pricing system. It even uses data from your phone's battery status to determine your willingness to pay. Namely, an empty battery means more urgency to get a ride (Martin, 2019).

Orica's target to transform human expertise into a scalable platform doesn't happen without data. Similar to many other companies, it started by boosting its digital capabilities. It collects data from its customers, such as the blast's goals, conditions of equipment at the site, the exact techniques and products used in the explosion and the outcome (Sherer and Cleghorn, 2018).

You also need to define, collect and refine the data that helps you reach your business goals. You produce the data by understanding what data you already have, automating data collection and leveraging partners' data.

Produce relevant data with these steps

These steps will help you produce the data you need.

Four steps for producing relevant data:

1 Clarify what data is currently used implicitly

2 Add technology to automate data collection

3 Leverage partners' data

4 Create rules for data sharing

---

1. Clarify what data is currently used implicitly

Building the data to support reaching your business objective should be done systematically to ensure that you capture all relevant aspects of the situation. Suppose you are using AI to improve a process or service that you are already offering. In that case, a crucial first step is to recognize what data is being used in the process currently. Some of the data being used might be explicit. For example, business decisions are partly based on market size and growth and other measurable variables. Likewise, medical doctors consider laboratory results when making their diagnoses.

In addition to explicit data, however, most human systems use vast amounts of implicit data. Humans observe their environment and use their background knowledge to make sense of the situation in which they are. For example, a business leader does not choose to enter a new market only based on market size and growth, but intuitively considers also various other variables, such as the political stability in the country, distance to the country from the home location, potential cultural differences and impact on firm morale. Likewise, a medical doctor forms an impression of the patient based on age, gender, general fitness, tiredness and other aspects that the doctor can immediately and casually observe.

An AI system should also measure the kind of implicit data that people use in various situations. Therefore, you need first to review the current operations and truly understand what data is being used. This requires both interviewing and observing the people doing the work.

Having catalogued the current data, you can complement this data with new sources that may increase decision accuracy and actions, for example, by extracting information on various events from news and social media using natural language processing.

Once you have obtained access to data, you have to ensure it is of high quality. Often data is incomplete, corrupted or includes mistakes. Data preparation is an essential process in making data useful for AI training. This involves detecting, correcting and removing corrupt, inaccurate and incomplete data.

For supervised learning (more on that later in this chapter), you need labelled data. You, therefore, need to mark data with a label to give it meaning. For example, assigning a set of symptoms a diagnosis is a label. Sometimes, you might have data, but if you miss labels, you cannot train the AI. You can define the labels yourself, but some companies provide labelling as a service; for example, Google (Green, 2020).

Finally, to make the AI genuinely able to learn, you need to make sure that you'll get access to performance data. For example, if a business AI makes decisions but does not have access to the results, it cannot improve over time. Likewise, a medical AI that makes diagnoses, but never learns if the diagnosis was correct, cannot become more accurate over time.

2. Add technology to automate data collection

Digital capabilities are a prerequisite for data collection. Smartphones powered the first wave of platforms as consumption devices but also as data-capturing devices. Without them, Uber, Delivery Here and so many other great platforms would not exist. The next wave of platforms, especially B2B, is driven by sensors of all kinds, which enable automation of data collection from innovative applications.

For example, Tesla's eight cameras capture video data with 360 degrees of visibility up to 250 metres of range (Tesla, 2020). In addition, 12 ultrasonic sensors detect hard and soft objects. Ultrasonic sensors send and receive ultrasonic pulses to measure an object's proximity. Tesla also has a forward-facing radar, which provides additional data and can see through heavy rain, fog, dust and even the car ahead (Tesla, 2020). You might not think of them as data-capturing devices, but the pedal and steering actions also produce data.

All the data from these sensors feed Tesla's AI system. And remember, hundreds of thousands of vehicles collect new data automatically, always when on the move.

Orica also illustrates this trend well. Who would have imagined a few years ago to connect blasts, data and AI? Orica thrives on technology to automate data collection. IoT sensors capture vibration, noise, air-blast, temperature, humidity, wind, dust and other parameters associated with the blasting operation itself. Furthermore, even a blast can't stop data collection. Rugged RFID tags track rock movements from the explosion. And after a blast, an image auto-analysis provides blast fragmentation data (Gill, 2018).

How could you automate data collection? Are there new sensors that open up new possibilities for data collection?

3. Leverage partners' data

Ramboll is a Danish engineering company. One of its divisions provides solutions for water and wastewater treatment. Its customers are water treatment facilities. Ramboll wanted to use AI to predict a water treatment facility's outcome. To do this, it needed permission from its customers to use the data for AI training. After a long process, the company managed to get the matter resolved, and permission was granted. Together with Silo AI, the Finnish AI Lab, the company built an AI solution to predict the quality of the water leaving from the water utilities. Among other things, the solution analyses how a water treatment facility reaches its environmental permit requirements.

Before AI, water management companies were focused on troubleshooting. Now, their attention can centre on predictive risk assessment and dynamic optimization of the facilities. A significant outcome of the project was that it's necessary to decide what data needs to be collected and at what level (Silo AI, 2019b).

This example illustrates the importance of working with partners, like customers, suppliers or other types of partners. Only by collecting enough data can you develop working AI. Besides, very often, data is not owned or gathered by a company but by its partners. Therefore, rules on how to share data and the rights of each partner are very critical. And you would be better off thinking this through early enough.

4. Create rules for data sharing

As discussed above, data often needs to be shared between partners or between customers and suppliers. However, companies are reluctant to share data as they worry that they give away something valuable. Data is the new oil, as they say. Managers might think that it's better to stock it than give it away for free.

To develop your own products and services, you might want to share operations data from the field with component providers and suppliers so they can serve you better. To do this, you need permissions and contracts from your customers. And thus, the terms and conditions for data need to be part of the sales agreement. The whole value chain needs to be thought through when it comes to data.

A concrete example of encouraging data sharing is the model terms of Technology Industries of Finland for data sharing. These terms are primarily intended to be used in companies' existing delivery and subcontracting relations (Technology Industries of Finland, 2019). The model contract includes a definition of data, terms for using the data, including third-party use, handling of personal information and liabilities.

Typically, companies cover data by nondisclosure agreements (NDA) or intellectual property rights (IPR) clauses. These can be very limiting as you can only use data for the specific use case and not for anything else. Therefore, a more generic approach is needed. The model terms allow for more extensive use of the data whereby you cut the cord between its originator and the end data user. Legal certainty is created so that nobody can present claims afterwards based on the data.

Clear data-sharing terms also shorten negotiation time and help to develop partnerships that promote the use of data in business development. Merging, filtering and cultivating multiple datasets between different ecosystem members create opportunities for innovation (Karjaluoto and Muranen, 2020).

When sharing data with third parties, companies should consider and specify what type of rights are granted to use the data. The rights granted also touch upon competition law. Suppose the rights are minimal, or the data is only shared with limited parties. In that case, courts might interpret this as restricting competition. Suppose data on prices and additional sensitive information is shared or can be derived from the data. In that case, this might, in practice, lead to a cartel (Schubert and Dayan, 2020). In a cartel, market participants collude to gain a competitive advantage. Thus, when creating rules for data sharing, consider also these legal aspects.

Continuous learning means acting better every day

You have created your vision, have identified where to start and defined your business goals. You then train your AI, deploy and update it based on new data and insights. In other words, you have created an AI-powered learning loop. Through the AI learning loop, you learn more of your business, develop new capabilities and thus realize you can expand the use of AI to new areas. Therefore, you should update your business goals.

The learning loop is never ending. For a single technical process, your learning might level itself. Still, then you can move on to the next process and update your business goals. You can expand to new industries and leverage your AI capabilities there.

This is what intelligent platforms do. They learn faster than incumbents. For them, building intelligence is an 'infinite game', as Simon Sinek outlines in his book (2020). To continue winning, you just need to act a bit better every day.

To illustrate continuous learning, consider Repsol, a Spain-based global energy and utility company (Ransbotham *et al*, 2020). The company has identified and started implementing over 190 digital transformation projects throughout its value chain. More than two-thirds of them leverage AI in one way or another. The projects substantially benefit Repsol and are essential to its business model. The project range varies from upstream drilling operations to activities performed at downstream service stations, such as personalized offers for customers.

In each area, AI and associated learning loops help Repsol perform the focal activity better every day. In the upstream, AI helps Repsol to improve productivity or drilling operations continuously. They analyse over 100 million data points per day. As a result, it has almost halved non-productive time in 30 drill sites. Thanks to continuous learning with AI. The AI system recognizes inefficiencies and their potential causes. Substance-matter experts then review the results and reflect on how to fix the situation best. The outcome is continuous improvement of the operations.

Closer to the end customers, AI and a learning loop help Repsol give evermore effective personalized offers to customers. The impact of these offers has been substantial: sales have increased as much as they would have if the company had added 3–4.5 per cent more service stations. This is a significant accomplishment. Each station would come with high costs. Besides, legislation and other factors constrain how many new stations it can open. The learning loop facilitates up to 400,000 personalized offers generated by the system every day and the AI-driven analysis of their impact. In this way, Repsol can make more effective offers every day.

Maximize continuous learning with these steps

You can initiate continuous learning in your organization by following these steps.

Four steps for maximizing continuous learning:

1 Train the AI offline

2 Integrate the AI solution into your current operations

3 Add human-in-the-loop

4 Update the AI model based on new data and insights

---

1. Train the AI offline

Before going to war, recruits go through extensive training. They are put in training situations that mimic actual events in the field. They learn to understand the meaning of various commands and enemy actions. They learn to make decisions based on the feedback they get during the training.

Similarly, you need to train your AI solution before deploying it in the field. Training the AI solution means that you first use the solution offline – such that it does not affect your business decisions or your employees' actions. Instead, you give data to the system, and it makes a decision based on the data. How good a decision it is, is then evaluated against a pre-specified criterion. Based on this, parameters in the algorithm get adjusted. This cycle is repeated until satisfactory decision performance is reached.

Key terminology for understanding AI

AI solutions consist of all the elements you need to build a working application integrated with your existing systems. An AI model is the brain of an AI solution. The brain is a good analogy for the AI model as most of today's AI is machine learning implemented with neural networks.

Neural networks imitate how the brain operates. Your brain consists of brain cells called neurons that connect through synapses. They transmit signals between neurons. Similarly, a neural network consists of nodes and their connections. The weights of these connections determine how different signals influence the output of the network. Data determines these weights. For example, by sifting through thousands of known financial fraud cases, the weights are adjusted so that the network learns to classify these fraud cases.

Learning happens in various ways. Most common are supervised learning, unsupervised learning and reinforcement learning.

Supervised learning is what most of today's AI models are based on, where the AI model learns from examples. Suppose you are training the AI to predict financial fraud cases in payment data. In that case, the data used for training need to have examples of fraud cases. These examples are called labelled data.

Another example is a data set consisting of received job applications and related CVs. They contain information about applicants' qualities. By labelling each application and CV with a label showing whether the applicant was selected for an interview or not, you have a labelled data set. By feeding this data to a machine learning model, the AI learns to pick the right people for the interview from new applications.

Unsupervised learning learns directly from data without prior knowledge of what the data is. This is useful when you are dealing with unknown events. For instance, in our example of financial fraud detection, unsupervised anomaly detection can automatically discover unusual data points in the dataset. In addition to anomaly detection, another common application of unsupervised learning is clustering. For example, suppose you don't know your customers.

In that case, you could cluster them with unsupervised learning based on common characteristics the AI would detect.

Reinforcement learning learns through trial and error. It observes the impact of action concerning a given reward. For example, in the classic Pong video game,
a reinforcement algorithm has only two actions. It can move the paddle to the left or right. The algorithm's target is to maximize the score, ie reward. A correct move increases the score, and a wrong move reduces it. Starting with random movements, it learns what works and what doesn't, thus learning how to play the game.

Reinforcement learning provides powerful opportunities for complex real-life problems. For example, teaching AI to control complex industrial processes could be done through trial and error in a simulated digital twin environment. A digital twin is a dynamic replica of actual equipment like a factory or forest machine. Chapter 7 explains this in more in detail.

Once you have trained the AI model, you evaluate its performance. For this purpose, you need a new data set, a test set. The evaluation process is typically iterative, testing several different models and selecting the best performing one. You don't always choose the most accurate one as the AI model needs to perform against other data sets. Sometimes, a model performs exceptionally well with the test data set but fails to perform in actual conditions. This is called over-fitting.

Tesla has several ways of training its AI models. First, Tesla can use data from cars driving without autopilot, ie learning from what a human does in different conditions and feeding it into the neural network. Second, it can compare autopilot results with human driving. And third, it can run new versions of the autopilot software in a so-called 'shadow mode', observing the difference from the current version and learning from it.

In the Tesla Autonomy Day (2019), Tesla's Director of AI, Andrej Karpath, explained how Tesla uses the fleet to train new situations like cut-ins whilst driving on a highway. With cut-ins, the target is to predict whether a car next to your vehicle will make a cut-in and then decide the best action. For example, if the cut-in is sharp, you might need to slow down or break forcefully.

Tesla requests the fleet to look at cut-in situations by central command. When observed, the data is sent back, in this case, a video clip of the situation. Humans then label this data, ie marked that these situations are cut-ins. Finally, the system trains the neural network with this labelled data set.

As AI becomes central to your operations, you might also need new systems. Most companies can get by with commercial tools, but some develop proprietary AI development environments. Uber could not train models larger than what would fit on data scientists' desktop machines. Furthermore, there was no standard way to store the results of training experiments. And it was hard to compare one experiment to another. Therefore, Uber developed its own AI platform to manage data, train, evaluate and deploy AI models (Hermann and Del Balso, 2017). Uber has trained more than 10,000 AI models for production with this system (Uber, 2019).

Orica trains its AI models with historical blast results. It has built a labelled data set consisting of objectives, the techniques and products used, and the blast outcome. Orica trains AI models with drilling data to determine ground hardness (Gleeson, 2020). This information is valuable in designing the optimum blast loading.

When you are integrating AI into your existing operations, you should remember the people. Consider Chapter 1 that discusses how to turn fear into energy. In particular, remember that decision-makers might feel threatened if AI replaces their judgement, and the organization's members' fears might cause rigidity and resistance.

2. Integrate the AI solution into your current operations

After the training and testing phases, you deploy an AI model into a production environment. The best is if you have an architecture that supports frequent updates. For instance, Tesla has a modular architecture with over the air update capabilities. Therefore, Tesla can deploy a trained AI model for the improved lane change into its large fleet of vehicles automatically and smoothly.

Many companies struggle with this as legacy IT systems are complex and monolithic. As data is buried into legacy systems, it's hard to access it to train and operate your AI solution. RPA (robot process automation) can help in this. It emulates human interaction with digital systems. So rather than humans getting the data, RPA will automate the task. Thus, integration with legacy systems becomes more manageable and cheaper.

A more complex challenge still is to get real-time access. Often, this might lead to a need to upgrade and modernize your IT systems. In the best case, your system also supports hardware upgrades, like Tesla.

Self-driving capabilities require real-time, low-latency and robust systems to work correctly and reliably in all situations. As Tesla's full self-driving AI models become better and more powerful, they also require more processing power. Tesla has developed its own AI processor, 'neural network accelerator', which provides 21 times improvement to image processing capabilities than Tesla's earlier hardware (Tesla, 2019). Enabled by the modular architecture, Tesla can retrofit vehicles already in use with the new hardware.

3. Add human-in-the-loop

Humans will remain at the centre of businesses, even in the age of AI and the platform economy. Almost all platforms have humans as users. As we have discussed, platforms use AI to propose the best course of action for the end-users. However, users are not just following AI's proposed actions mindlessly. They can actively take a stand on the quality of the AI's proposals, especially in B2B platforms.

For example, when a healthcare platform proposes a patient diagnosis, a doctor will check it and then approve, reject or modify it. By capturing this feedback, the AI can learn and improve. In AI terms, they are labelling the data. Thus, we should think of humans as our best partners for AI development. They can label data as part of their everyday work. People and machines collaboration is more powerful than automation alone.

The learning AI system's ultimate value comes from professionals' feedback as they validate or reject the AI models' proposals. This way, the knowledge from various professionals is captured, building a continuous learning loop that will benefit the whole value chain and improve customer satisfaction (Nykänen, 2019).

But just looking into the final suggestion by AI is not enough. For example, healthcare professionals need to be aware of the data points that led to the suggested diagnosis. Explainable AI can visualize factors behind AI's proposal. This helps to understand the logic behind the AI model's neural networks. This is additional information for a doctor to decide if the AI's suggestion should be accepted or rejected. No more black boxes.

Uber is also experimenting with human-in-the-loop systems. Uber Eats is a popular food delivery service. Its user orders food with the app that delivers the order to a restaurant for preparation. An Uber driver or other delivery partner (bike or pedestrian) picks up the meal and delivers it.

A critical factor in Uber Eats is to predict the right pick-up time for the order. The delivery partner should arrive at the restaurant when food is ready for pick up. This depends on two factors, food preparation time and delivery partner travel time. Machine learning predicts both of these based on various signals.

As there is no incentive for the restaurant to provide the actual preparation time information at the time of an order, the system needs to predict it. The prediction uses information like the average food preparation time for the past week and for the last 10 minutes, time of day, day of the week and order size. The type of food also has a significant impact on the preparation time. You can prepare a salad faster than cooked items. Therefore, natural language processing extracts the menu information. This data is one factor for the AI model to predict food preparation time (Wang, 2019).

But just leaving this to machines was not enough. Researchers started to explore what causes Uber Eats deliveries not to be completed. The study led to adding a human-in-the-loop approach in the courier app. Through a questionnaire, couriers can share valuable insights like how busy the restaurant is and where its entrance is located. This information fills in the gaps in Uber's sensor data and improves delivery time prediction AI models (Baker, 2018).

In summary, consider the following aspects when deploying AI models:

1 How do you deploy AI models into the system – can you automate the process like Tesla?
2 Is your infrastructure up to date – processing capability, data management, latency and other requirements?
3 Do you need to build in modular hardware upgrade possibilities?
4 How are your business processes changing, and how can you ensure users like employees, customers or suppliers adopt new ways of working?
5 Do you need to add human-in-the-loop?

4. Update the AI model based on new data and insights

Once the AI model is trained and deployed, new data is fed into the system, producing results. For example, continuing on with our Uber example, let's assume we predict the estimated time of arrival (ETA) when driving a given route. Once the ride is complete, the actual time of arrival is known. This can be compared to the estimated time and fed back to the system to improve the next prediction. Of course, this example is simplifying a lot as several factors affect the time of arrival. However, as the number of rides is large, statistically, this becomes meaningful. The system can also determine which factors influence the outcome most.

By analysing and learning from actual events based on its predictions, Uber learns to fine-tune its AI systems. The learning loop drives the system performance to become more robust, reliable and accurate in matching demand and supply.

The learning loop is a virtuous circle where the system's use produces new data that is used to improve the system. Let's look at how Tesla is using the learning loop in more detail. After training, the Tesla system is run in shadow mode. The new software runs in the vehicle but does not steer. The actions of the new AI software are compared to what the car is doing. Based on these differences, AI is trained further.

Tesla is collecting new data processed in the cloud to train new versions of the self-driving software based on neural networks. This makes the software better step by step. In this way, the software could learn to write code to automate driving (Efrati, 2018). Again, we see a learning loop in action.

In 2019, Tesla acquired a startup, DeepScale. Its technology improves the speed and efficiency of convolutional neural networks. These networks recognize cars, pedestrians, bicycles and other objects. Self-driving cars need the information of surrounding things to determine where to move next (Lee, 2019).

As more and more customers use Orica's Blast IQ and input more of their own data, the company will build a significant enough dataset to develop more powerful machine learning models to provide even better services. In practice, this is changing the business model of the company, creating a competitive advantage.

Similar to Orica, many manufacturing companies have successfully built expert services. This type of company has to think about how they teach their top-level expertise to a machine and enable sales globally, creating a new market for themselves. Artificial intelligence makes it possible to duplicate knowledge and remove the constraints created by a place.

Key takeaways for your organization

To win in business and fight newcomers, you need to be a bit better every day. Learning loops power your organization to do that. If you are an incumbent, your new competition is running faster with an AI-powered learning loop. They rapidly improve their value creation and efficiency. Thus, to stay in the game, you need to do the same. Start learning today by defining your goals, assessing your data and building the first learning loop.

Start from business goals

- How could AI-enabled learning transform your company? What new businesses can you create?
- Have you checked what is feasible for AI vis-à-vis your business vision?
- Which processes and activities could you first improve with the AI learning loop?
- How will you update your business goals based on the learning with AI?

Produce relevant data

- What factors do your managers and employees implicitly consider when making choices?
- How could you use technology to measure relevant activities and outcomes in your current operations?
- Which other companies have data that could benefit your activities? Could you collaborate with them?
- What rules will you use for sharing data with other companies?

Maximize continuous learning

- What data will you use to train your AI system offline?
- How will you implement AI in your current operations?
- In which parts of the process do you need human input or judgement?
- What practices will you use to update your AI models?

CHAPTER FIVE

Open up with an algorithmic handshake

Do you want to expand your ecosystem and business with new services? It is not enough to innovate internally. You need external parties to create compelling services for your customers. This is especially true for platforms.

Opening up your platform requires acknowledging you cannot do everything alone. This is often a challenge for the leaders of successful organizations who have gotten used to having power and control.

An effective way to open up your platform is an application programming interface (API). We would claim that you cannot engage with partners without APIs. APIs provide a mechanism to share data and functionality, enabling computer programs to interact. APIs define how software programs communicate with one another. For example, APIs determine what one software can request from the other, how it should make its requests, what data format it should use and other technical factors.

With APIs, you can extend your reach and innovation capability with no human interaction. Instead of trusting on a human handshake and negotiations, you trust computers to perform the handshake by automating the work. With APIs' help, your platform partners' software communicates directly with your platform and/or other platform members. In this set-up, algorithms check if the collaboration is appropriate and beneficial and coordinate the needed actions.

Opening up with an *algorithmic handshake* is more efficient and scales better than approaches relying on human contact. With APIs, computers rather than people can manage the work. And as you get partners to onboard to your platform faster, your network effect gets stronger.

In this chapter, we will explain how you can:

- Define your business goals for APIs.
- Develop APIs as products and define them with a business model.
- Take a lifecycle view of APIs.

Application programming interfaces

APIs are modern-day contracts as they allow algorithmic handshakes. Partners just need to fulfill certain conditions and use the defined instructions. After that, they can connect and use your platform – no need for face-to-face interactions, negotiations and handshakes. Everything happens automatically and virtually.

APIs define routines and data structures for interaction. Through APIs, third-party applications can communicate with your platform. APIs make platform implementation details abstract. Therefore, partners don't need to know how your platform works internally. And you can make internal changes without impacting your partners. Of course, if you change the API itself, that can have drastic impacts on your partners. Therefore, you need to manage APIs as products.

KONE is a global leader in the manufacture of elevators, escalators and automatic doors. KONE also maintains over 1.4 million elevators and other products worldwide. It realized the importance of partners several years ago. KONE's mission is to improve the flow of urban life. To do this, it needs more than just elevators and regular maintenance.

KONE's customers seek new solutions and services. For example, robots for in-house logistics. Or robots could serve as receptionists. Also, there are mobile apps that guide our way in complex buildings. For example, an app knows your destination in the building, shows you the way, and orders elevators in advance for you. Just walk in and the elevator moves to the destination floor automatically. KONE APIs make these experiences possible. With APIs, KONE can multiply its innovation capability as APIs create an ecosystem of partners.

Through APIs, partners get access to the functionalities and data of your platform. You notice the benefits of APIs soon. For example, Google Maps APIs allows developers to embed Google Maps into their applications. Instead of Google building all kinds of applications, partners like Yelp use the map API to power their applications. With APIs, companies can concentrate on the value-adding part.

But do you believe others are up to the job of driving innovation through the use of your platform and APIs? Fear of losing control hinders the progress of building and adopting APIs. The challenge for leadership is to turn fear into energy, as we discussed in Chapter 1.

For many of us, John Deere brings to mind a green tractor and childhood memories from a farm. John Deere was founded over 180 years ago. Still, it has been transforming itself from a machinery company into an intelligent platform during the last 10 years.

Can you do farming while relaxing on a bench from your front porch? Thanks to APIs, this isn't that much of a fantasy. It's already been 10 years since John Deere started building APIs to enable its machines to connect with various applications. The first API platform started with just a couple of developers. The platform team and management focused on making these APIs work. They needed to figure out what data to share, how to get a yield map and share it with various software companies, to enhance John Deere's unique advantage (SuccessfulFarming, 2020). In other words, the John Deere team was attempting to define the value that data and the functionalities exposed through APIs bring to their customers.

But success with APIs and developers isn't to be taken for granted. In its early days, Twitter APIs were free as it needed to drive traffic to its service. Then, it limited the free usage and charged for the API. Twitter also started to control more of what applications developers could create based on its API. Twitter was unclear in its communication to the developers resulting in backlash and developer relationships soured (Dellinger, 2013). In 2015, its CEO Jack Dorsey even apologized for mistakes in its API programme and promised renewed attention on developers (Mersch, 2016). This example highlights that you need to reflect on how you implement and manage your APIs.

Start API development with the audience and value in mind

APIs can drive innovation and expand your platform reach and use. But you should not launch them lightly.

Often, companies focus on the technical capabilities of a platform. As a result, they just offer those capabilities through APIs without thinking why. However, one should always start from the audience and business model. Who is the audience, and what do they want? What value does your API generate to the audience? Under what business terms are you willing to make your platform available?

Being clear on your goal helps define your developer program. Streamlining efficiency differs significantly from driving innovation. Your target sets requirements for developer outreach, marketing and other activities.

When talking about users, keep in mind there are two types of users for APIs: developers and end-users. Developers are the ones who code applications using your API. They are interested in technical and operational details. End-users use applications powered by the API. They define your business requirements. You should therefore listen to them when deciding what type of APIs you should develop.

Why and how do APIs generate value?

In the following section, we will explain why you should create APIs to speed up your platform development.

> The reasons you should develop APIs:
>
> 1 Unlock innovation
>
> 2 Expand reach
>
> 3 Streamline processes
>
> 4 Monetize data

1. Unlock innovation

APIs empower your customers to design their own experiences. Instead of forcing customers to use your platform through your own applications, you let the customer develop applications and create the user experience. You accelerate the adoption of your platform and unlock innovation.

KONE started developing smart building solutions about seven years ago. One of the first innovations was just a simple app to call the elevator. KONE realized there was market demand for new solutions. However, the difficult integration process hindered progress. At the time, digitalization was not a core business for KONE.

Jukka Salmikuukka is director of strategic partnerships at KONE. He explains how the situation changed. Back then, one start-up asked if KONE had APIs. It wanted to make a visitor management system. And the system should be able to call an elevator.

> I thought there has to be a smarter way to get more solutions out. Therefore, the idea of an ecosystem crept into my mind. Why not build an ecosystem with different solution providers? They would fill the gaps that we cannot do ourselves. (Salmikuukka, 2020)

Hence, he realized that an open API was the missing link. With an API, KONE could connect third parties to its business system. It has two APIs to create new experiences for customers.

The first is related to service robots in hotels. Robotise is a German-based delivery robot company that provides hotels with a robot called Jeeves. Jeeves delivers room service 24 hours a day. It allows hotel operators to provide a rich set of products as there is no need to store them in individual rooms. Moreover, there is no need for costly investments in old-fashioned minibars.

KONE's service robot API allows tracking of the service robots' movements. It facilitates immediate corrections to any incidents. Through the API, applications can integrate with elevators. For example, robots deliver guests' luggage to hotel rooms autonomously. Another example is cleaning or security robots, who can move without human supervision.

KONE's second API is the elevator call API, which allows building owners to create smart building applications. These include remote elevator calls and traffic analytics. It integrates with building access management systems. Hence, it enables seamless, more secure and efficient people flow.

For example, REDI is a high-rise residential condominium in Helsinki, Finland. Tenants enter their home building with a key that connects to smart access solution. After that, the access solution calls an elevator. As a result, it will be ready when the user arrives at the elevator lobby.

KONE is building APIs because it wants to stay ahead. A central assumption in KONE's strategy is that smart buildings are here to stay, and the need for new solutions will continue to grow. The smooth flow of urban life is more important than ever today. In some instances, people flow will be integrated with energy management systems. This will help to manage peak energy loads. It will also enable new services for building users.

For instance, BlindSquare is a navigation app for blind or partially sighted people. BlindSquare uses KONE's APIs to integrate with elevators. Through the API, the app can call the elevator. Thereafter, the elevator relays information to the app. The phone says 'elevator door opens' so people know when they can walk on.

To find the right escalator, a visually impaired person needs to touch the handrail. This causes safety risks as a hand might get trapped between the handrail and balustrade. Therefore, KONE plans to expand the API to escalators. Through the API, escalators would relay their status to the BlindSquare app. Then, the app directs the visually impaired to an escalator going in the right direction: 'the two escalators on the right go up; the one on the left is coming towards you' (KONE, 2019).

KONE's APIs have enabled third parties to innovate around KONE's core products. Think how this could inspire you to think about how other companies might innovate your core offering. If you provide APIs for them, they can implement various value-adding elements that complement your core product or service. It's a clear win-win.

2. Extend reach

In addition to expanding your core offering with additional innovations, APIs can make your product or service more available for users. By making your product or service also available within another product or service, you are facilitating enhanced user experience and access to your product or service.

In 2014, Uber launched its API, which enabled other applications to use Uber's platform capabilities. For example, an OpenTable user booking a restaurant reservation could request an Uber ride straight from the OpenTable application.

OpenTable used the Uber API to request the trip and passed the destination address to the Uber platform. This increased the customer value for OpenTable users. They could handle all their administration needs related to eating out in a single place. And it enabled Uber to scale faster by distributing its service through other apps.

APIs expand platforms' reach and scale. Rather than marketing and distributing yourself, your partner will help and create a significant multiplier for scaling. Often this happens by integrating through APIs to legacy systems.

Such an approach to APIs has enabled Flexport to expand radically. As noted in Chapter 3, Flexport is a modern freight forwarding company. It operates a digital platform that connects cargo senders to ships and receivers, enabling more efficient global logistics. APIs have a central role in this model: Rather than trying to make everybody use their platform, Flexport enables the integration of their platform into other applications through an API. The Flexport API allows you to interact programmatically with Flexport's freight data. Data through the API include purchase orders, prices, quantities and terms.

The Flexport API enables customers to organize shipments from their in-house software with minimal customization. Customers stay on their own platform and communicate with Flexport via the API (Wintrob, 2017). The benefit of this approach is that customers can use familiar applications with no need to change their usage and still access the advanced capabilities Flexport has built. For example, customers can track when goods arrive at their warehouses and tell retailers when to expect re-stocks. The API also alerts them about delays in real-time.

John Deere is also building on legacy systems. Many vendors have already developed business management systems for farmers. Farmers would not replace their existing systems for a John Deere specific business management system. Therefore, it makes sense for John Deere to provide a particular API to connect existing farm management systems into its services.

3. Streamline processes

APIs also help you improve the efficiency of your current and future operations. They can replace various manual processes in both B2C and B2B transactions. They also provide real-time visibility to multiple operations, reduce latency and improve responsiveness (Adobe, 2019). APIs create new value by stimulating innovation and extending your reach. But they also help you do what you are already doing more efficiently and reliably.

CASE STUDY   John Deere's APIs for farming

Today, you cannot operate a farm without data and information. For example, the status of soil moisture is critical to maintaining optimal growth conditions. Work planning requires the status of the current harvest and what's planned next. Maximizing yield calls for the right mix and timing for irrigation and fertilizers and understanding weather conditions. And if something goes wrong and you lose your harvest, you need data to prove your insurance case.

To enable all this, machines need to be connected. John Deere's API-based approach helps to do that and streamline farming processes.

By analysing its customer needs and processes, John Deere saw the opportunity to expand its value chain position. Instead of just selling tractors and other machines, it could help farmers to improve their business. John Deere's management realized its current machines collect data others could use to innovate new applications. API was the missing link.

John Deere turned their products into an open ecosystem by developing API for data transfer and other purposes. Now farming activities like tilling, digging, picking with tractors, excavators and loaders produce data that improves operations with development partners' help (Akana, 2014). APIs also allow flexible connection of new devices like irrigation systems into the ecosystem.

As a result, John Deere streamlines processes for farmers and creates a network effect. Every new farming machine and application connected to the system produces new data that enables more accurate predictions and insights.

To illustrate APIs' benefits for efficiency and reliability, consider KONE's APIs for management and service purposes. One of them is the KONE Equipment Status API. It provides equipment status information. With it, building owners can integrate status information into their management systems.

For example, maintenance operators manage many types of buildings. These include large residential and office buildings, railway stations and airports. They want visibility for their elevators and escalators. It helps them to assess if the building is working and people are behaving normally. If there are disruptions, they can respond rapidly as they get the information in real time.

Building owners also use KONE's service info API. It provides access to the elevator data for asset or building management systems. Hence, it removes the need for point-to-point system integration. It also reduces manual work and human error. Building management systems get information on open and completed service orders, call-outs and repairs. They can, therefore, maintain full situation awareness and schedule the right actions at the right time.

4. Monetize data

Through APIs, you can expose and monetize data that other companies need. To get started, analyse your internal data and how it is used or could be used. Assess also external data you could collect. Then consider how you could combine external and internal data to create value for your customers or other partners. Once you understand the value creation potential in this way, it's time to define APIs that will provide access to and process these data. Once you have that, you can consider who would be most willing to pay for the data and how you might charge them.

An excellent success case of data monetization is The Weather Channel (TWC), now part of IBM. It transformed itself from a media company with a declining business into a growing platform through APIs. It powers numerous applications with its weather data.

Develop APIs as products and define a business model

APIs could provide many benefits. However – just like with any invention – its potential does not necessarily equate to success. Many technologies have high potential, but only a subset of them turn into actual innovations that become widely adopted and indeed generate value. To avoid the fate of creating an API that is technologically perfect but used by no-one, manage them like products.

You should view APIs as products that empower developers to expand your data and services into new apps, experiences and business models (Endler, 2017). And products need product management. APIs are no exception.

Product management guides the lifecycle of API by defining its strategy, roadmap, features, positioning, pricing and marketing. APIs also need a business model and an explanation of the terms on which you are ready to make your APIs available.

Partners develop their products and services on top of your APIs. For them to commit to doing so, they need an understanding of your API strategy and positioning as well as pricing. Any changes in APIs have significant implications for your partners. It can break their experience and, in the worst case, lead to significant losses.

Create successful APIs through these steps

Once you know why you need APIs, you need to create and develop them. Follow the four steps described below.

How to create successful APIs:

1 Create internal APIs

2 Assess customer needs

3 Define API roadmap and communication plan

4 Define API business model

---

1. Create internal APIs

When developing new recipes for cooking, you try the meals yourself before you offer your meal to others. In this way, you learn what works and what does not. Similarly, when developing APIs, an excellent way to start is to define first internal APIs.

Amazon started with internal APIs with a strong mandate from the CEO. Bezos issued an 'API Manifesto'. It began with a statement: 'all teams will henceforth expose their data and functionality through service interfaces' and that 'teams must communicate with each other through these interfaces' (Kramer, 2011).

Similar to Amazon, the elevator company KONE uses the same APIs as partners for internal development. Finland's largest retail bank OP Financial Group has also developed internal APIs and uses them for all development work. Hence, there is a keen interest in making them work well.

Starting from internal APIs is valuable for two reasons. First, they help to create a modular architecture and decouple different development efforts from each other. This is important because the modular architecture reduces interdependencies between elements that could create various complications. If there are interdependencies, changing one thing requires changing several other things. In contrast, when there is modularity, different elements can be changed without changing other things.

When you develop APIs for internal use, you learn to create modularity. You are unlikely to get it right on your first try. Instead, you understand which features each API should have so that they work well together. Hence, besides improving internal efficiency, you learn to make better structured APIs before offering them externally.

Secondly, developing internal APIs helps you assess your company's strengths. You learn what value-adding services you can offer via APIs.

To define what APIs you could offer, you can start by tearing down your business. You tear down your business functionalities and analyse each piece. What capabilities or data do you have? Would they be useful for partners?

For example, machines used in agriculture like tractors have enormous amounts of data. To be useful, you need to get the data out of the fleet. John Deere developed a machine data API that retrieves machine data so other systems can use it.

To get started with internal API development, you could consider:

- What internal services are used by several units in your organization?
- Which of those services are sufficiently standardized?
- Which of those services are genuinely value-adding?

Answering these questions builds a list of possible internal services to be offered via APIs. In the next step, you could start technical specification of the APIs and start experimenting if and how they work. The experimentation feeds to their further development.

1. Assess customer needs

Understanding your customers' needs helps to define the right type of APIs for them. What problems are your customers trying to solve? Can APIs actually help? Sometimes, providing an API to suppliers and partners might help to serve your customers better.

For example, farmers and their systems need to understand field conditions, such as soil moisture levels and environmental conditions. Sensors collect data that is continuously logged, stored and transmitted. Applications can access this data through the John Deere field connect API and help farmers to make better decisions.

In the manufacturing industry, customers and other partners benefit from access to product lists, product details, instructions, spare parts information, repair information and store locators. Companies can use APIs to make these readily available. Custom APIs can provide customer-specific information such as product purchase and maintenance history (Glickenhouse, 2017).

To understand what your customers need, assess their business through interviews. Interview three to five customers. What processes do they have, and how could data or functionality you can offer help to improve those processes? Interview also your customer's customer. This helps you understand what drives your customers' business and how they produce value to their customers.

2. Define API roadmap and communication plan

Treating APIs as a technical concept only leads to failure. Of course, a technically well-designed and robust API is needed, but it is not enough. APIs need a strategy and roadmap like any other product.

Your API strategy describes how you achieve your business goals related to APIs. It includes clear targets, priorities and resources. API strategy aligns the organization with your goals. It also defines a strategy for your customer and developer outreach.

An API roadmap consists of API features and their timing. It shows what features the development team is building, including resources for each development item. It helps to prioritize development items against your strategy and customer needs.

Many companies and their business depend on your API. Therefore, you cannot change APIs without managing your stakeholders. Without early warning and proper communication, a change might result in fatal damages to your partners and your reputation.

For example, KONE APIs have product owners. They manage the API lifecycle and roadmaps. For every development partner who uses APIs, KONE has a community manager. He or she communicates API changes and other information to partners. In addition, they collect insights from partners to improve APIs.

To define your API roadmap and communication plan, you should continuously consider and re-evaluate:

- What APIs do you want to create?
- How much development time and resources are needed for each API?
- How will customers benefit from the APIs? What is the overall value added by the APIs to your platform?

- In which order should you launch the APIs?
- How and when should you communicate about the APIs to your customers?

3. Define business model

Suppose you want to build an application that analyses tweets' sentiment for your company. In that case, you need access to relevant tweets. Twitter search API provides that. For the first seven days, it's free. After that, you need to pay for access. Twitter has a freemium business model. Get started without paying, but if you want complete access to better data, it costs you.

The business model defines how you make money with your APIs. The right business model depends on your goals for APIs. Some of the most common business models include free, freemium, revenue share and paid models.

Free business models fit well with goals like accelerating innovation and extending reach. For example, Facebook would like to become a standard login provider for different services to connect users to its ecosystem. Therefore, Facebook's login API is free. For manufacturing companies, free APIs can simplify sharing product information.

Revenue share models encourage other companies to build applications to drive business to you. For example, Skyscanner shares part of its revenue with apps or websites that bring revenue above a certain threshold. Skyscanner's live pricing API provides 'up-to-date pricing information for a specific route on a specific departure and arrival date', allowing easy price comparison and selection (Skyscanner, 2021).

With paid APIs, developers pay for their usage of the API. The fee could be based on a number of API calls, the amount of data or a flat monthly fee. For example, KONE's API is free for developers but not for building owners. Building owners buy elevators from KONE. For its API usage, they pay a monthly fee. The value from APIs for them is to bring advanced services to tenants and other users.

For KONE partners, APIs are free. Partners develop solutions, for example, a delivery robot. They sell these solutions directly to building owners. When a delivery robot needs to use an elevator, it calls the API. KONE is responsible for making sure the API works. Furthermore, it ensures the elevator responds in the right manner.

So, a KONE customer buys a solution from a partner and API usage from KONE. Partners develop the API integration. In exchange, KONE promotes them through marketing. In addition, it maintains a catalogue of partners and their solutions.

At first, KONE wanted to sell the partner solutions. The business model would be a revenue share. However, the company's core sales skills would not scale, especially if KONE would get hundreds of partners. Therefore, partners sell their solutions themselves to customers. But KONE markets them. Sometimes both the partner and KONE approach customers together. KONE can also create tighter co-operation. Especially if solutions sell and suit the offering very well.

The trade-off KONE needs to remember when considering how to charge for its APIs is how it influences the network effects related to value creation by the APIs. On the one hand, KONE wants to make revenue from its APIs – if they were free for all platform stakeholders, KONE's revenue would be zero. On the other hand, a fee reduces building owners' likelihood of adopting the API. This, in turn, reduces the number of buildings where partners and developers can benefit from the API, making the APIs less valuable for them. And if partners and developers find KONE's APIs unattractive, they do not provide value-adding services that could be used via the APIs. For building owners, this would mean that adopting the API would not improve their building in any way. Hence, they would have no incentive to adopt the APIs.

Similarly, when you are considering the pricing for your API, you need to think about how you want to develop your ecosystem over time. In particular, how long should you prioritize ecosystem growth instead of revenue? The faster you start billing people for the use of your APIs, the less likely others are to adopt them. But the probability is never zero, so the right answer is not necessarily that you should always prioritize growth over revenue.

Take a lifecycle view on APIs

After you have developed your API and launched it to the market, developers will come, right? Not so fast. You need to market and manage your API. To do this, you should have a comprehensive developer program, and a lifecycle view. As your API evolves, you need to manage changes to not alienate your developers with drastic changes that might make their apps and services unusable.

Key terminology for understanding APIs

There are many commercial and technical considerations when developing APIs. To make your APIs successful, you need a *developer program*. It provides marketing and technical support for your APIs. Its customers are developers and programmers who might come from small start-ups or large corporations.

Developer programmes provide resources such as API documentation, release notes and roadmaps. A developer programme produces marketing content, including feature and partner announcements to drive awareness and attract an audience. And a good developer programme educates its audience through tutorials and workshops. Developer programs usually charge a membership fee (Williams, 2020).

On the technical side, developer programs provide software development kits (SDKs). Typically, an SDK includes one or more APIs, programming tools, software libraries and documentation (Glas, 2020). By offering SDKs, companies make it easier for third parties to develop applications that use their platform capabilities. Instead of leaving design choices to the developer, SDK provides ready-made solutions resulting in more consistent third-party applications.

SDKs are designed for specific platforms. You need an Android SDK toolkit to build an Android app and an iOS SDK to build an iOS app. Or even a Facebook SDK to build apps that work in Facebook. Think about Stripe, a payment platform. It would like its service to be used by as many merchants as possible. Therefore, it provides SDKs for different programming languages and application platforms like iOS and Android.

From the business point of view, SDKs simplify things for developers. Still, you can also provide APIs without SDKs, leaving the implementation for developers. This trade-off depends on the sophistication of the developers.

Taking a lifecycle view on APIs means taking the following steps.

Four steps for API lifecycle management:

1 Market your APIs

2 Measure and manage

3 Be consistent and have patience in developing your ecosystem

4 Consider industry API platforms

1. Market your APIs

According to the ProgrammableWeb API directory, there are over 23,000 APIs (ProgrammableWeb, 2021). Many APIs fail for the simple reason that nobody has ever heard of them. To avoid that fate, you need to market your API.

You should be clear about who your target developers are. Who should use your API? Once you know that, it's easier to build a marketing programme. Developer marketing activities include informative developer pages, social media campaigns, email lists and developer events.

If you are serious with APIs and building an ecosystem, committing to a developer event is necessary. And it needs to be a long-term commitment. Most well-known events include Apple Worldwide Developers Conference, Google I/O and TrailheadX Salesforce Developer Conference.

But industrial companies also have their own developer conferences and programmes. For example, Develop with Deere of John Deere. Since 2014, it has brought together software companies, dealers and agriculture service providers. Today, the John Deere developer programme supports hundreds of different software companies from various industry sectors: insurance, farm management, aerial imagery, financial profitability, soil sampling, to name a few (SuccessfulFarming, 2020).

In 2020, John Deere had their largest developer conference, Develop with Deere, in its history. Over 700 people and 120 different software companies participated (John Deere, 2020).

2. Measure and manage

After development, launch and marketing, you would think enough of APIs. But to succeed with APIs, you need to take a long-term, full lifecycle view. The work has only started.

How do you know your API is having any impact? Of course, like in any business, by measuring it. Connect your metrics with your business goals. We can outline four different targets for your API: unlock innovation, extend reach, streamline processes and monetize data. Each of them requires different metrics (Boyd, 2017).

For innovation, measure how many partners have built new applications on top of your API and how often they use the API. If you target extending your platform's reach through third-party apps, measure the number of new customer sign-ups through these apps.

To streamline processes, measure how many partners have connected their systems to your platform through APIs. And how much time and effort were saved avoiding costly integrations.

To measure your impact in monetizing data and your platform functionality, use metrics like revenue based on your pricing model and growth rates.

Measure and track also your marketing impact. How many developers visited your site, churned, signed up to your developer programme and started and finished their applications using your API.

APIs evolve and change. And ultimately, they become outdated, and you need to depreciate them. You need to manage different versions of APIs and keep track of backward compatibility. For this, API management platforms are a useful tool.

The wider your API is used, the more your customers' business is affected when you update the platform. If you change API and your partner applications won't work, you are in trouble. Not only are users angry, but developers are disappointed and will flee your API programme.

Thus, building and making changes in a backward-compatible manner is a good practice. If you break your API, then communicate it well in advance. Both to business and technical stakeholders so they can prepare.

Even goals and metrics in place might not guarantee success. You still need transparent governance and an organizational model. Who can decide and what? How to prioritize resources, resolve conflicts and decide on roadmap changes. Some organizations have a centralized API centre of excellence reporting for CTO, but you should also consider other models (Iyengar *et al*, 2017).

3. Be consistent and have patience in developing your ecosystem

John Deere's API and developer journey started in about 2010. KONE likewise started figuring out their platform ecosystem several years before launching the first APIs in 2018. Building trust and commitment takes time and patience. It's crucial to be consistent to earn the trust of your organization and partners.

KONE is facing firm pressure to stay consistent over time due to the elevator industry's characteristics. Each building is unique and requires significant investments. Therefore, partners need to sell their solutions to building owners. These might have building-specific requirements.

The smart building market differs from the smartphone market. There is no app store and access to millions of customers. And delivering a new solution can take up to three years. Moreover, the lifecycle of buildings is uncommonly long. After 10 years, 99 per cent of buildings still exist. However, the use can change quickly. That is why the retrofit market is essential. The elevator business is relatively concentrated. Therefore, even one player providing open APIs is beneficial. It makes development easier for partners.

It's hard to develop APIs and an ecosystem for this type of market. But KONE saw the market need and took a long view on innovation. They started with focused experiences, tested and learned.

KONE has tried to make it easy to join its ecosystem to accelerate development. As the number of partners grows, it creates a 'honeypot' effect. Over time, the goal is that KONE customers and other partners see the increasing value. The ecosystem creates a positive lock-in effect.

However, creating an ecosystem is not easy. It also means changes to the sales process. For KONE, instead of selling elevators and their features, it is selling a future-proof platform. The platform, together with partners, provides solutions for customers' problems.

While KONE's need to stay consistent over time is particularly strong, any API developer faces the same pressure. No-one wants to work with a partner who changes the specifications and rules frequently. That would lead to wasted work. Hence, consistency should be one of your key priorities.

In addition to acting consistently and changing your business model, building an API ecosystem requires reimagining the sales process. Furthermore, it means training sales to rise to the challenge.

New sales approaches might include a fresh approach to managing your brand. For example, KONE's partner solutions are not KONE branded. Partners deliver innovative solutions to the customer. Thus, they are responsible for the solution from an end-to-end point of view. KONE ensures that APIs work.

In case of problems, customers might contact KONE regardless of the cause. Therefore, KONE and partners need to have solid processes on how to work together. The target is to solve the issues without delays.

Companies should manage the ecosystem brand and service experience. For example, KONE measures the quality of its partner solutions regularly.

Each partner candidate must pass through a KONE partner onboarding process.

Security, privacy and quality audits are part of the process. This ensures that partners create quality solutions that meet the quality bar. When in use, KONE monitors its API service quality around the clock. Also, it expects partners to do the same for their solutions.

4. Consider industry API platforms

Although John Deere has gathered impressive momentum with its developer programme, it is still just one company. Not every farmer buys a John Deere tractor, and thus not all data is utilized by John Deere developers.

Leaf was founded in 2018 to connect hundreds of agriculture data sources from different companies to address this problem. The Leaf API integrates with several companies like John Deere, AGCO, Trimble, New Holland and over 50 public data sources (Manning, 2020). So, developers need to only integrate with the Leaf API to access data from all these brands in the future.

Through the Leaf API, developers have access to standardized, aggregated agriculture data. The data includes machine data for various brands, field boundaries, as well as field images from satellite, drone and airplane providers. Field boundaries can be imported, exported and synced across multiple agriculture service providers.

Leaf is an example of an API-first company. It is an intermediary layer that connects industry participants. API-first means API is the primary business model and way to access the company's core services.

Another example of the API-first model is Stripe. Stripe API enables the fast provision of payment functionalities to your application and ensures a consistent payment experience. Stripe created an API-first company by smart design choices driving the business. It has a comprehensive SDK and documentation to make the life of developers easier. It automated the sign-up process to avoid any delays in taking Stripe API into use. After signup, a developer could immediately integrate the API into their application and testing in a sandbox environment. (Sandbox is a safe, isolated environment for running new, untested software code.) And finally, the Stripe business model with no upfront or monthly fee encouraged the API's take-up. And the price of the API was the same for all card types despite the varying costs. Simplicity is beautiful and drives adoption (Levine, 2019).

API-first might be the direction also in the building and elevator industry. KONE also services competitors' elevator products. Therefore, it would have the interest to use its APIs even there. But KONE's competitors have established their own APIs. Hence, there might be a need for a third party like Leaf to integrate different APIs.

Key takeaways for your organization

An algorithmic handshake automates connections to your platform participants. The easier it is for third parties to connect to your platform, the more value they create for you, and vice versa. API-powered algorithmic handshakes are efficient and scale fast. While technical, API-development should be driven by your business goals, you should be strategic and manage them like any product.

Start from business goals

- How could APIs transform your company?
- What do your customers need?
- Which processes could be streamlined by APIs?

Manage APIs as products, including business model

- What internal services could you offer through APIs?
- What is your API roadmap?
- What metrics should you use to measure API success?
- What would be the optimal way to monetize your APIs?

Take a lifecycle view to APIs

- What type of developer programme should you build?
- How will you market your APIs?
- How will you ensure consistency over time?
- Is there a need to develop industry-level APIs?

CHAPTER SIX

Create the unexpected

G oogle was a search and advertising company when it moved to mobile operating systems. A few years later, it dominated 80 per cent of the mobile market with Android. Who would have expected that at the time? Only Google understood that it needed to evolve as a company and move to new businesses to stay relevant.

Google's example shows how traditional industry boundaries are disappearing. New competitors seem to come from out of the blue. However, they actually result from Intelligent Platforms becoming the norm for how successful companies re-architect themselves.

Intelligent Platforms are entering new businesses by redesigning the entire value chain and being bold enough to challenge the status quo. Therefore, they are creating the unexpected and breaking current definitions and boundaries of traditional industries.

Such quantum leaps in business performance depend not only on continuous data-based improvement but on *conceptual insights*. Such insights involve inventing a new category, business model or a way of conducting business – ie a platform expansion. Data analytics and reasoning within the current scope of your business alone will never lead to conceptual insights; you also need creativity and out-of-the-box thinking. In this chapter, we outline several methods that you can use to spark conceptual insights:

- Outside-in: starting from market trends and opportunities.

- Inside-out: starting from your current strengths and assets.
- 'What if we bought': considering how you could leverage another company's strengths.

In the end, we will provide simple psychological techniques that can help boost your creative thinking while generating conceptual insights.

Conceptual insights need creative thinking

Chapter 3 described the three fundamental steps required to develop a platform: start with focus, refine and expand the platform incrementally and create an engaged community.

While analytics have allowed platform companies to improve their current service substantially, the firms have also made more radical moves and initiated new businesses. Those moves were based on increasing understanding of changing customer needs and creative recognition of novel opportunities. They were, in part, enabled by the successful existing platform – like Amazon Web Services and its AI capabilities, which became an asset that companies could leverage in novel ways into new industry verticals.

We call these discontinuous, radical changes in the platform scope conceptual insights – creative ideas about leveraging a platform in a novel way or bringing it to a new customer group. Conceptual insights often emerge through experimentation which enables proactive expansion.

For Uber, conceptual insights have included switching from limousines to regular cars and expanding into delivering packages and meals. These changes qualify as conceptual insights because no matter how much Uber had analysed the data on the earlier, simpler version of their service, they would never have come up with the subsequent idea. For example, even if Uber could model and predict demand person transportation and trip duration with 100 per cent accuracy, the idea of getting into package delivery would still not present itself. Instead, the platform leaders had to think outside the current service to find new areas to expand.

Amazon's conceptual insights have included the various ways it expanded its product categories, including third-party sellers; the launch of the Kindle reading device; the introduction of subscription services; and the expansion into cloud services. For example, Alexa is a voice-controlled intelligent assistant that works with Amazon Echo and connects to various smart home applications. Forgot to lock the door? Just say: 'Alexa, lock door', and it's done. Alexa launched in 2014, and by the end of 2018, Amazon and its hardware partners had sold over 100 million Alexa-powered devices (Bohn, 2019).

Even before 2014, Amazon had been working on natural language processing and voice control. Amazon engineers must have understood that voice-recognition capabilities were attaining near-human levels, soon exceeding 90 per cent accuracy. In 2013, voice searches on Google picked up, with a clear upward trend (Meeker, 2016). As voice recognition became quicker, more comfortable and more accurate, people began to regard it as a viable user interface.

This combination of a market trend and new technical capabilities allowed the emergence of a unique opportunity. For example, if consumers began searching with voice, Google's dominance over search could be weakened. Seizing the moment, Amazon expanded into the new category of intelligent assistants – an evolution of its Amazon Web Services platform.

These moves are conceptual insights because comprehensive analyses and optimization of Amazon's book sales would never have led to the introduction of other product categories or third-party sellers. Again, the leaders of the platform had to come up with creative ideas to expand the service.

For Facebook, conceptual insights have included introducing the news feed, the 'Like' button and event groups; improved advertising models; Facebook Messenger; and many other features and enhancements. Again, while data analytics were essential for measuring the quality and performance of the introduced features, the idea of creating them came from the creative efforts of the company's members.

There are several methods you can use to create conceptual insights. The common thread in all of them is that you first develop a wide variety of ideas. Then you select the best ones for further refinement and implementation. You need a large idea pool of ideas because you can rarely know in advance which ones will be successful. You need to explore many avenues before you find the right way forward.

To generate plenty of ideas, you need methods to enhance creativity in your thinking. Still, the ideas you come up with should be plausible. An effective way to generate a myriad of ideas is to start your thinking process from a range of starting points and then expand into novel directions from each of these starting points. As long as you ground those starting points in reality and your company's current situation, you have a high enough chance of attaining plausible insights and executing them.

Outside-in: starting from market trends and opportunities

A straightforward way to generate ideas for conceptual insights is to look at current market trends and opportunities. For example, Amazon assessed customers' changing habits in terms of using voice search. Usually, you can see specific market segments or categories that are growing. Specific technological trends might also create new opportunities. Recognizing such external developments, you can consider how your company could seize the emerging opportunity.

Our example of Amazon Alexa illustrates the potential of connecting new technologies with your current core. It was not only Amazon's technical development of Alexa but also its ability to market and deliver Amazon Echo, which drove the platform's growth and success.

Develop outside-in conceptual insights through these three steps

To develop your own outside-in conceptual insights follow the steps below.

Develop outside-in conceptual insights through these steps:

1 Monitor and reflect external trends

2 Consider analogies from other industries

3 Explore potential partnerships

---

1. Monitor and reflect external trends

To recognize market trends, you need some consumer and market intelligence of your own. However, you can also benefit from general market reviews published by trade journals and websites. In the early stages, you need not analyse the opportunity down to the last decimal point.

Moreover, AI is making it easier to follow and discover trends. AI can process thousands of documents with lightning speed, find patterns in text, cluster them and spot emerging trends. For example, a company's internal market intelligence team could collaborate with an AI-company to develop a tool for scanning magazines, discussion forums and other online channels. The tool would create a report of emerging trends, and the market intelligence team would prepare a monthly report for the senior executive team.

One trend that has been growing in recent years is online shopping. One of the first implications to consider is that someone has to deliver goods purchased online to the consumer. Many postal and package delivery companies grew with this trend and rode the increasing demand. Uber used it to reach a conceptual insight. Its expansion into package delivery with UberRush happened because Uber's leaders recognized the need for fast delivery. Uber's CEO's vision was to turn Uber into a logistics company. First, UberRush focused on local retailers, but this niche didn't scale fast enough. Then, Uber applied the insights into another vertical, restaurant delivery, and launched UberEats.

It's a similar story with technology: you can often recognize trends based on general reviews of technologies and their opportunities. While your research and development experts may excel at the details of your company's current technologies and their forthcoming generations, when it comes to conceptual insights, it is often technologies outside your company's core that provide the next opportunity. Or, more precisely, it is the combination of your company's current core with the activities enabled by the new technology.

To develop ideas for conceptual insights from recognized external trends, you can run a focused project that has the following elements:

1 Create a 10–20-slide presentation about your core market and technological trends that could relate to your company's business, whether directly or indirectly.
2 Run a workshop where you first present the trends and then ask participants to elaborate on them and their potential implications for your business and industry.
3 In the second part of the workshop, ask participants to form potential ideas for how your company could connect to the trends or apply the associated technologies in new ways.
4 Collect all the ideas and dedicate teams to further refining the most promising ones.

2. Consider analogies from other industries

Another starting point for outside-in conceptual insights is drawing analogies with other companies. You learn from a company that has faced a similar situation in another industry. You look at that company's choices and actions and consider the analogous actions for you.

A snack company, for example, with a valuable brand that sells its products to a retail channel might consider Disney to be a suitable analogue. Disney used to produce movies and TV shows, then sell them to distributors (mainly cinemas and TV networks). However, realizing the increasing importance of online streaming, Disney has launched its own streaming service. It is hoping to leverage its brand value and unique content to attract many consumers. If Disney succeeds, it will bypass a traditional distribution channel and have the possibility of opening up its platform to third parties: the movies and shows streamed via Disney's online service need not be produced by Disney itself. Disney benefits as more consumers subscribe to the service, attracted by the amount of content available, and pay a monthly fee. In addition, Disney gets access to real-time data on consumers' viewing preferences and patterns at a second-by-second level. It can now see precisely which scenes or lines cause viewers to hit pause or change channel, for example, enabling the development of evermore appealing shows.

Analogously, the snack company could consider creating its own platform. Besides selling its snacks via retailers' online stores, it could launch its own online store. If the brand was strong enough, there was the possibility to provide unique products exclusively via the online store, and the pricing was attractive, enough consumers might find the online store worth visiting. The traffic would also allow the company to open the online store to other snack companies. It could become a new hub for buying snacks online. Again, the benefit would come from taking a cut from other companies' revenues. Additionally, the company could continuously improve its products and services by analysing the increasing volumes of real-time consumer data.

B2B companies could also expand using the Disney analogy. Consider the case of a factory machine manufacturer that sells spare parts for its machines. Currently, the firm operates like the traditional Disney – it produces the parts itself, and someone else handles the distribution. It could, however, seek to create a platform that would allow it to sell its machinery and parts to factories directly. Later, it could also expand the platform to include other manufacturers' products and related items too. In this way, it might create a highly value-adding service for the factories, a 'one-stop-shop' for all machinery and spare parts. This 'one-stop-shop' would provide a highly efficient sales and distribution channel for other manufacturers.

The manufacturer would enjoy a revenue share of the sales via the platform. But even more importantly, it could collect and analyse all transactions and other data to continuously improve its products and services. This example closely resembles Tetrapak with its spare parts and services marketplace, which we discussed in Chapter 3, 'Focus your actions to create fans'.

Using analogies to generate novel ideas is often the most creative approach but also the most difficult. Analogies lead to more creative ideas than other techniques. They increase creativity because they remove the starting point for thinking from your company's current core. Instead, you start from a different company's perspective and thus further away from your own company.

As our examples illustrate, your analogies can come from your industry or other unrelated ones. However, wherever you look for analogies, pay attention to profound relevance. A company might seem superficially relevant because it has operated in the same geographical location or used the same technology. However, this analogy might be irrelevant on a deeper level because the company has a fundamentally different structure to its business.

For example, before its ultimate scandal, Enron ventured into the broadband business due to lousy analogy use (Gavetti et al, 2005). Enron's leaders saw that the broadband industry had similar characteristics as Enron's other businesses. They believed that the wholesale business model they used in the gas and electricity business would be highly profitable in the broadband industry. They based their reasoning on superficial similarities between the industries. Both had fragmented demand, changes in industry structure due to technological and legislative changes and high capital intensity. However, Enron's leaders missed that, unlike gas and electricity, they could not trade broadband bandwidth efficiently via similar standard contracts. Furthermore, in the broadband business, a substantial additional cost came from building the last mile to customers' sites. Consequently, Enron's broadband venture made disastrous losses.

To use analogies to develop conceptual insights, follow the sequence illustrated in Figure 6.1 below:

1 Reflect on what is most relevant in your current situation. For example, is it channel or technology transition, legislation change or some other force that creates new opportunities for your company?
2 Identify relevant analogies for your company. Create a list of 10 companies from at least five different industries that have faced a similar situation to

the one your firm faces now and have taken actions to resolve that situation. Map the analogue's steps and consider what the analogous actions for your company would be.

3 Select the three best ideas for further development. Think further how it would look if your company took analogical actions.

FIGURE 6.1   Use analogies to come up with novel ideas for your current situation

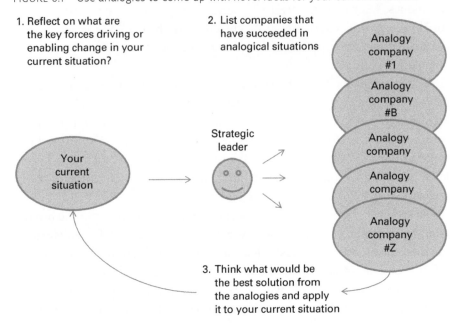

1. Reflect on what are the key forces driving or enabling change in your current situation?

2. List companies that have succeeded in analogical situations

Analogy company #1

Analogy company #B

Analogy company

Analogy company

Analogy company #Z

Your current situation

Strategic leader

3. Think what would be the best solution from the analogies and apply it to your current situation

3. Explore potential partnerships

Another way to start from 'somewhere else' is to consider how your company could partner with another company. In such a set-up, you would combine the partner company's stakeholders and capabilities with your own. This combination would allow you to imagine new potential services. Ideas can come from imagining how combining two products or services that are typically not considered complementary could create something unexpected and value-adding.

Amazon has also grown through this approach. In 2018, it created a joint healthcare venture, Haven, with J.P. Morgan and Berkshire Hathaway to improve care for its employees. It's a non-profit venture. A conceptual insight behind this approach is that there is a growing trend of rising healthcare costs and disconnected services that are not focused on patient outcomes. Creating a joint venture that focuses on customers – ie internal employees – helped Amazon create a new offering and learn new capabilities to expand its offering in the healthcare sector in the future.

Leading shipping company Maersk created a joint venture with IBM, known as TradeLens. The venture used Maersk's core knowledge of the shipping industry to create a global trade platform built on the blockchain. Their target was to reduce the cost of worldwide shipping, improve visibility across supply chains and eliminate inefficiencies stemming from paper-based processes.

The TradeLens platform connects shippers, carriers, ports, terminal operators, logistics providers and freight forwarders. They share actionable supply-chain information in real time, for example, shipping milestones, cargo details, trade documents and sensor readings. Tradelens also features APIs that enable external partners to use its data, foster innovations and build applications or connect legacy systems, as discussed in Chapter 5, 'Open up with an algorithmic handshake'.

Partnerships can also speed up technology adoption and enhance innovation capabilities essential for developing your company or platform. For example, many companies are reimagining their design paradigm with mixed reality (a combination of real and virtual worlds with a headset or other screen). Volvo and Boeing are among them. They both have partnered with Varjo, a Finnish start-up we discussed in Chapter 3, 'Focus your actions to create fans'. Varjo enables designers to review photorealistic virtual objects in mixed reality using real-time lighting sources from the physical world. This technology creates an immersive new design environment transforming the way designers work. It's possible to simulate much more realistic designs earlier on in the design process. It also enables the collection of data from human interaction with the design.

To develop conceptual insights by considering potential partnerships, you should:

1 Name a handful of potential partner companies.
2 Consider what capabilities and stakeholders these companies have.
3 Imagine what you could do together if you combined elements from your capabilities and stakeholders with theirs.

Inside-out: starting from your current strengths and assets

A second approach for developing conceptual insights is to begin by looking at your existing skills, capabilities, assets and resources. Ask yourself how you could use them in novel ways, to do something radically different.

Apple, for example, has long had the capability to develop devices of ever-increasing functionality and ever-shrinking dimensions. It also has an attractive consumer brand. Having developed the iPod music player, Apple realized it could add phone functionality and turn it into a smartphone. But before that, it tested the waters with a partnership. Motorola Rokr E1 phone connected to Apple's music service iTunes. Steve Jobs launched it in 2005 but wasn't happy with the quality and design and was also afraid of the phone eating into iPod profits. But with new insights, it moved to develop the iPhone (GSM Arena, 2019).

Once the iPhone existed, a natural way to leverage the capability still further was to make smaller iPhone-like devices – ie smartwatches. Thus Apple's prevailing skills and capabilities carried it into a new product category.

Apple's conceptual insights opened up new horizons for the firm. Before the iPhone, it operated in the computer and portable music device categories but then moved into radically different ones. With smartwatches, Apple entered another new category that had been dominated by specialists such as Garmin, Polar and Suunto.

These moves also enabled Apple to expand its platform. iPhone enabled the App Store ecosystem. Apple Watch provided an additional sub-platform that attracted new kinds of actors, such as developers of health and exercise apps, to join the ecosystem.

The critical point is that Apple had ideas and development projects related to many of these areas and ultimately focused on those it saw as most promising. Similarly, you should consider how you could use your firm's current strengths and capabilities for various purposes and then select the most promising ideas for further development. Changing consumer habits and timing should also be critical factors in your decision-making.

Develop inside-out conceptual insights through these steps

To use the inside-out approach, follow these steps.

Develop inside-out conceptual insights through these steps:

1 Identify your current strengths and how you use them

2 Imagine alternative uses for each strength

3 Choose a winning combination

1. Identify your current strengths and how you use them

Often, companies take their unique strengths for granted. You do so because you see your company applying its strengths every day. You may forget that what is easy for you can be difficult for others. Hence, it is useful to reflect and record what strengths your company has.

Executive teams can drive this process. For example, in 2003, the Amazon executive team analysed the company's core capabilities during an executive retreat (Miller, 2016). Initially, they focused on an e-commerce company's natural capabilities, such as fulfilling and shipping orders. But after digging deeper, the team realized Amazon was also running reliable, scalable, cost-effective data centres. The idea of offering this to third parties was the spark for what would become known as Amazon Web Services, launched in 2006, and cloud computing was born. Competitors were slow to respond, allowing Amazon to build a significant market share.

In your firm, you could assign a project team to identify your company's current skills, capabilities, assets and resources. The team should identify the 10–20 most essential items.

Keep a broad perspective on what constitutes strength. If you operate in a specialized industry, your advanced technological skills may not feel special because your competitors also have corresponding skills. In reality, you might still be one of the few companies in the entire world with those skills. You could leverage the skills in various products and services outside your current market category.

The classic VRIN framework (Barney, 1991) can help you in seeing what constitutes a strength:

- Valuable: does this resource or capability generate value? For example, clean water is valuable, as are uranium and cutting-edge programming ability.
- Rare: is the resource or capability rare or common? Uranium and cutting-edge programming abilities are rarer than water and, hence, more likely to be your strengths.

- Inimitable: can it be copied? It's easy to copy, eg a business location, but challenging to replicate cutting-edge programming ability.
- Non-substitutable: can it be replaced with something else? You can replace tiles with concrete for most tasks, but not programmers with lumberjacks.

You should also consider how the potential strength behaves in the platform era: does the strength get more potent due to network effects or not? For example, having numerous users in a particular service gets evermore valuable due to network effects, whereas uranium does not have a similar quality.

2. Imagine alternative uses for each strength

Once you have recognized your strengths, consider alternative uses for them. You can use any strength in several ways. For example, clean water can be used for drinking, making soda, showering, shooting at people in crowd-control settings and so on. Likewise, what you have could be used differently than how you are using it today.

Tesla's 2015 expansion into the home energy storage market illustrates how a company can find new uses for its strengths. Tesla had developed significant competence and capability in the production of car batteries. Simultaneously, the home energy market needed solutions to store energy from solar panels, which only generate electricity during daylight hours. Tesla developed a battery solution, Powerwall, as well as Tesla Solar Roof.

Although such solutions were already available, Tesla's branding, design and solution architecture excited consumers and energized the market. Four years after its launch, Powerwall has grown significantly, and CEO Elon Musk has even predicted that it could ultimately be more significant than Tesla's electric car business (Korosec, 2019). Many people's view is that Tesla is actually in the distributed energy business.

Amazon's entry into healthcare is a combination of the outside-in and inside-out approaches. In 2019, it acquired Pillpack, an online pharmacy specializing in filling prescriptions for patients who take multiple medications daily. (This wasn't the first time Amazon had considered entering this market. It had already invested in Drugstore.com but subsequently sold its interest.)

Amazon's initial approach was outside-in, starting from the vast market opportunity presented by the market trend of rising healthcare costs. Annual spending on prescription medication at US pharmacies is $397 billion, almost 50 per cent of which is captured by the top three pharmacies: CVS Health, Walgreens and Express Scripts (Campbell, 2018).

However, Amazon also thought inside-out. With the Pillback deal, it acquired a back-end software system called PharmacyOS, which automated prescription renewals, billing insurance, getting authorizations from providers and sending out notifications (Farr, 2019). Connecting this to Amazon's current strengths – ie shipping, the Prime programme and the possibility of marketing Pillback to customers of the Amazon-owned Whole Foods Market – created an opportunity to accelerate Pillpack's growth in the pharmacy market.

To proceed in practice, task the team you appointed for identifying the strengths to come up with at least five different uses for each skill, capability, asset and resource. In this way, you will get at least 50 potential new activities that your firm could perform with its current strengths.

Make it a requirement that at least half of the new activities are in a different product category or market, such that you ensure a wide variety of radical ideas, not just incremental refinements of your current business.

Group the potential activities into themed sets so that you can combine ideas that overlap with each other. Select the most promising ideas for further development.

3. Choose a winning combination

One plus one can be two, three or seven. It depends on which 'ones' you choose to combine and how you combine them. Hence, it is not enough to identify new, valuable ways for using your strengths, but you should also consider various alternative combinations. Which strengths should be combined? Which potential uses of each strength would create the most value?

In retrospect, Apple's progression from the iPod to iPhone and the Apple Watch seems natural or inevitable. In reality, the company considered different ways to use its strengths. It could have used its capabilities in computing, consumer electronics and branding for entering or creating many categories – for example, automotive, augmented and virtual reality, or home automation.

Some of the possibilities Apple considered were closer to being ready than others, and the company, therefore, implemented them faster to the market. Still, it also thought how it could combine the strengths in novel ways in the longer term.

For instance, Apple executed a project to enter the automotive market. In 2014, it hired more than 1,000 engineers to join a project called 'Titan' to build an electric car, but the project switched its focus to AI and self-driving car software in 2016 (MacRumours, 2021). In June 2019, Apple purchased Drive.ai, a self-driving vehicle start-up, to boost its efforts. It is also still rumoured to launch a self-driving electric car by 2026 (Gurman and Bloomberg, 2021). While Apple's plans for this category remain unclear, the story so far already highlights that leading platform companies often experiment and pilot new ideas before expanding their platform scope.

In practice, you could look at the list of potential uses for your current strengths. Then consider various combinations of the uses and imagine what you could create with each combination. Some of the combinations might very well be useless or silly, but a fraction of them might create novel, unexpected value.

'What if we bought... ?'

A third way to create the unexpected is to consider potential acquisition targets. Imagine how buying them could lead to new kinds of platform elements. This mental exercise provides more random starting points for your thinking as you list attractive prospects from various industries.

KONE, for example, attempted to buy a rival Thyssenkrupp to consolidate the elevator industry in 2020 but ultimately concluded the risks were too high. However, it could also consider acquiring various other types of companies and reflect on the implications for its product and service ecosystem.

KONE could also look at security companies such as Securitas. In its 2021 strategy, KONE states that it manages people flows in buildings with elevators, escalators and doors. The acquisition of a security firm could push this service model to a new level. KONE would also be more actively monitoring who is entering the premises, preventing unauthorized access and ejecting intruders. This expanded approach would allow KONE to handle all people flows in buildings and develop user interfaces to manage them in smarter, more proactive ways.

Three ways to use the 'what if we bought' model

Consider the following approaches to using the 'what if we bought' model to develop your conceptual insights.

Three ways to develop conceptual insights through 'What if we bought':

1 Transform the target company with your capabilities

2 Use a target company's platform capabilities to transform your business model

3 Buy platform capabilities to transform your business model

1. Transform the target company with your capabilities

If you already have platform capabilities, you can use them to transform other companies and their industries. By definition, most industries are behind the leading ones, such as media and telecommunications, in digitalization and 'platformitization'. Hence, if you are a forerunner, you have several great opportunities in other industries.

In 2017, Amazon made its biggest acquisition: the Whole Foods Store grocery chain for US $13.7 billion. It had experimented with bricks-and-mortar shopping with initiatives such as Amazon Fresh, a grocery delivery service, and physical Amazon bookstores opened in 2015. Reflecting on these ventures, Amazon had realized that while physical stores will never disappear, the future of shopping will be a blend of online and offline experiences. Amazon had already carried out a 'what if we bought' analysis of different alternatives and considered buying Whole Foods, but ultimately decided against it (Soper and Giammona, 2017).

However, when a new opportunity emerged and Whole Foods entered a bidding round with other potential acquirers, Amazon stepped in and clinched the deal (Business Insider, 2017).

Since completing the acquisition, Amazon has leveraged its core and integrated its Amazon Prime membership programme into Whole Foods stores. Whole Foods rolled out pick-up and delivery services through Prime, providing home delivery within two hours. Whole Foods stores also serve as locker pick-up points for Amazon's online customers, extending the firm's platform.

With Whole Foods on board, Amazon also gets data from offline shopping, creating new insights for platform development. Combining this with data from its online platform creates a more substantial dataset for training AI and machine-learning algorithms. This improved learning enables better targeting of products, and thus Amazon's learning loop gets even better.

Now, let's turn this example upside down. If you are 'Whole Foods', would you be able to find a company with platform capabilities that could help you to transform your business model?

2. Buy platform capabilities to transform your business model

If your platform capabilities are not yet developed, you can accelerate your process by acquiring them. If you do this boldly, it helps you transform your business model and become a true forerunner.

In January 2020, Visa announced its intent to acquire Plaid for US $5.3 billion. Plaid is an API-first company. It makes it easy for people to securely connect their financial accounts to the apps they use to manage their financial lives through its APIs. With this move, Visa, already a match-making platform, was planning to position itself as an evolving Intelligent Platform with a new foundation to grow, leveraging its scale for Plaid to grow even faster. The approach remained feasible even after antitrust authorities forced the acquisition into a partnership.

Plaid started as a pure consumer payment API. It built APIs that connect consumers, traditional financial institutions and developers. Its focus on security has gained the trust of banks, developers and users. Initially, it provided access to bank data for developers. Plaid's Quovo acquisition 2017 extended it to the investment and lending space. Right after the acquisition, it launched a new API, Investments, based on Quovo. The new API powers customers' apps by fetching their investment data (Miller, 2019).

As we can see, Plaid followed the four steps we outlined in Chapter 3 to build its platform. It started with a tight focus on developers and users with a payment API and gradually expanded its scope organically and through M&A. The conceptual insight of understanding that it could grow into investments and lending led to the acquisition of Quovo. Visa, in turn, expanded its platform capabilities by partnering with Plaid.

As another incumbent in a traditional industry, the American retail chain Target has been threatened by increased online shopping. While Target has strengths, such as its established inventory and operations, transforming into an online store is not trivial. In addition to the need to create an attractive e-commerce site and internal processes, customer logistics become a significant challenge. Consumers want their items home delivered. And they often buy from the store that delivers fastest.

To speed up the transformation into an online store, Target acquired Shipt for US $550 million in 2017 (Target, 2017). Shipt is a platform company focused on same-day delivery. Shipt has a fleet of shoppers, one of the key stakeholders on the platform. At the time of the acquisition, they already had 20,000 shoppers engaged in the platform. They pick up items from various retailers ordered by consumers, who are another key stakeholder in the platform, and deliver them to the consumer.

By acquiring Shipt, Target could strengthen its position in the platform. Instead of being just one retailer among many, it now became the primary choice. In this way, Target is becoming a multi-sided platform where it connects the producers of various products to consumers via shoppers.

By late 2020, Target's transformation was on track, despite the challenges created by the pandemic (Target, 2020a). Indeed, the pandemic had made the online channel more critical than ever and boosted the company's profits. According to the chairperson and CEO of the company, Brian Cornell, they experienced 'unprecedented market share gains and historically strong sales growth, both in our stores and our digital channels' (Target, 2020b). Highlighting the importance of the Shipt platform, Target also announced it would add another 100,000 shoppers to Shipt ahead of the winter holidays of 2020 (Target, 2020a).

Sometimes you do not need to have a clear business case for the capabilities you are acquiring. Instead, you may recognize a potentially relevant capability and buy a company with such a capability. When you do this, you assume that once you start integrating the new capability with your existing operations, you may, ultimately, come up with the idea that will create the unexpected. For example, Facebook's acquisition of Chainspace in 2019, a UK-based blockchain start-up founded by researchers from University College London, followed this logic (Cheddar, 2019). Chainspace has been developing smart contracts using blockchain – ie contracts that activate without human involvement when certain conditions are met. In the future, Facebook might integrate smart contracts to its offering directly or use Chainspace's capabilities in some other ways.

Now reflect: what companies could provide valuable new platform capabilities for your firm?

3. Buy out the competition to reinvent yourself

Sometimes, 'what if we bought' moments come from perceiving direct threats to your platform. A good example is Facebook's acquisition of WhatsApp. Facebook already had its messenger service, and it could well have tried to compete with that. But given WhatsApp's astronomical rate of growth, Facebook acquired it for a mind-boggling US $19 billion. Facebook had concluded that people will always use a range of different messaging applications.

The same insight lay behind its acquisition of Instagram, the popular social photo-sharing service. Realizing that people use multiple photo-sharing social media services, Facebook continued to expand its service features alongside those of Instagram – and emulated the so-called 'stories' feature from SnapChat for good measure. In both these cases, Facebook preserved the acquired platforms' independence and did not merge them with Facebook's core, thus sidestepping the integration woes (and frequent failures) that often befall companies that acquire a competing service.

With WhatsApp and Instagram, Facebook acquired new data sources, which it could use to understand consumer behaviour better and monetize its consumer base. This data-based learning would accelerate the development of its learning loop, which we discussed in Chapter 4, 'Create a learning loop'.

However, access to the new data also raised questions of privacy and data ownership. Should Facebook really be able to use the data from its newly acquired services elsewhere? Facebook had planned to share and use data from WhatsApp in its core, but this was put on hold due to regulatory investigation (Lunden, 2018). However, in 2020 Facebook again considered integrating Facebook, WhatsApp and Instagram infrastructure, potentially opening the door to data sharing between them and better monetization of the combined user base (Isaac, 2019).

Are there potential competitors that your firm could acquire? How would you benefit from combining the operations? Or would it make more sense to keep the companies separate?

Manage people and emotions to stimulate creativity

So far, we have considered the thinking patterns and information-related aspects of finding conceptual insights. To make the four techniques more useful, you can also support them with psychologically informed practices that ensure that team members notice all relevant information and build up their ideas through collaboration.

Stimulate creativity through these four techniques

1 Boost creativity with material practices

2 Manage emotions to boost creativity and develop conceptual insights

3 Create sufficiently diverse teams

4 Postpone idea selection – and then do it systematically and critically

1. Boost creativity with material practices

The first step in all the approaches we have described for developing conceptual insights is collecting some sort of information: external, internal, analogies or acquisition targets. Often, when companies are performing strategy projects, they collect these kinds of ideas into PowerPoint presentations, which are then viewed individually (on devices) or collectively (in workshops). The problem is that people only see each slide for a moment and rarely return to it multiple times or see it alongside other slides simultaneously. Yet, creative thinking, idea elaboration and novel connections are more likely if people return to the same inputs multiple times and think in an iterative, non-linear way. Hence, it's helpful to create a *physical library* for your insights – not just a digital repository. With new tools, you can also turn your physical library into a virtual one, like a showroom.

To create your library, take the following steps:

1 Collect various types of input materials in visual form and mount them on the meeting room walls you're using for the insight process. This ensures that all team members get sufficient exposure to all inputs and recognize potential connections with inputs that seem distant from one another.

2 Ensure people visit the library room(s) multiple times and do at least some of their work in this room(s). This helps team members think and cumulate their thinking. Besides, social interactions in the room can spark creativity.

3 Enable the recombination and recategorization of ideas by making items moveable (for example, by writing them on sticky notes). Provide lots of

blank paper and flip-charts so people can jot down new ideas. As everyone sees how the thinking is progressing on the walls, the team's collective process becomes more cumulative and more likely to produce new value instead of fragmented or overlapping ideas.

4 Take frequent photographs of the walls to capture all iterations.

2. Manage emotions to boost creativity and develop conceptual insights

The mental processes of you and your team members generate conceptual insights. Emotions substantially influence human mental processes. So, you also need to manage the emotional side of the process. There are three fundamental emotional states that you need to generate in the different parts of the process.

First, when creating new ideas, you need to generate positive emotions. People think more creatively in a positive state, as the association chains in their brains are longer when people are in a positive mood (eg Fredrickson, 2001). This means that they can connect more distant data points and see patterns between activities, enabling them to go beyond the obvious. Also, a positive emotional atmosphere creates social dynamics where people feel safe to voice their unfinished ideas, which is necessary for elaborating them collectively (Edmondson, 2019).

Second, when evaluating ideas, you need to change the positive climate to a more critical or even negative one. In the evaluation stage, you need to pinpoint your ideas' weaknesses, and mood-congruent thinking in a negative mode helps in this. Brain research has shown that people think more logically and focus more on details in a mild negative state (eg Phelps *et al*, 2014).

Third, when seeking to elaborate and refine the ideas, you need to facilitate empathy, such that the perspectives of all relevant stakeholders are sufficiently integrated into the conceptual insights. Being empathic when interacting with stakeholders makes it more likely they will share honest and relevant information with you, making the concept more appealing to them. At the neurological level, intentional empathy facilitates the activation of mirror neurons. This helps you or your team members see the concept from the stakeholders' perspective (eg Praszkier, 2016).

You can manage the emotional climate through the following means:

- **Your example.** Display the emotion you need your team members to experience. Research has shown that emotional contagion from leaders to team members is powerful, and you can leverage this mechanism to your advantage (eg Barsade, 2002).

- **Music.** Play music that arouses the needed emotional state before meetings and during breaks (eg Hunter and Schellenberg, 2010).
- **Food.** When you need positive emotions, make sure that people have enough energy and are not irritated due to hunger.
- **Venue.** Pleasant locations and facilities support positive emotions, while slight discomfort activates more negative moods. For example, you could brainstorm on beanbags, then sit on hard benches for evaluation.

3. Create sufficiently diverse teams

Different people think in different ways. Creativity results from combining diverse ideas in novel ways. Hence, one way to increase creativity – and develop conceptual insights – is to have more diverse people in the team(s) developing conceptual insights.

You should consider diversity from multiple perspectives – not just gender, age and ethnicity. An essential but often neglected factor is the diversity in the people's experience (eg Healey, Vuori and Hodgkinson, 2015). This includes their education, work history and other adventures. Do not hire people with a similar profile, such as an Ivy League MBA with more than five years of management consulting experience, but select people who come from very different places. Different schools, companies, positions, outside the typical business sector and so on.

In addition, consider the mix of personalities and thinking styles. You want fast thinkers and slow thinkers. You want extroverts and introverts. You want big picture people and those who are into the details. It is their combination that makes them find novel connections and create the unexpected.

4. Postpone idea selection – and then do it systematically and critically

So far, we have discussed different methods for creating a long-list of potential ideas for conceptual insights. The next step is to narrow it down and choose which ideas you will refine further.

First, you need to define the relevant criteria for evaluating the attractiveness of the ideas. For example, when considering ideas for AI-powered platforms, the criteria used could include:

- Attractiveness to different sides of the platform: does the potential multi-sided platform provide value for all the intended sides?
- Can the chicken-and-egg problem (how to get both sides of the platform joined) be resolved, and if so, how?
- Overall business potential.
- Technological and legal feasibility.

Second, you need to systematically apply your criteria to the ideas that are being evaluated. Typically, the first step in this task is to assign an analytical team to collect relevant data and model them. In addition, you might need experts' qualitative opinions, discussions with potential partners and clients, and experiments.

Third, you can use social practices to evaluate your ideas in more detail and dig deeper into facts and figures. One technique that works well in the later stages of idea evaluation is formal debates: you assign one team to defend an idea and another team to oppose it. As the teams debate, they identify further aspects of the idea relevant for its potential and feasibility. Besides, an active debate energizes the process in a way that formal analyses and presentations do not.

Key takeaways for your organization

Creating the unexpected is a fundamental step for your business. It is about transcending current industry boundaries and shifting to the next level. It's about moving away from static, old-school strategy toward radically more dynamic strategizing. To do this, you need conceptual insights that define where you shall move next. There are three critical methods for developing conceptual insights. In addition, regardless of the method, you should lead the psychological dynamics of your team and organization to stimulate creativity.

Outside-in

- What new opportunities are external trends creating for your company?
- Could you do something analogical as another company has done?
- Could you create something valuable and unique by partnering with another company?

Inside-out

- What are your current strengths?
- Could you use your strengths in novel ways and combinations?

'What if we bought?'

- Could you transform a target company with your capabilities?
- Could you transform your business model by acquiring a platform company?

Leading the psychological dynamics

- Do you have practices that optimize the psychological dynamics for creating conceptual insights?
- Are your teams diverse enough?

CHAPTER SEVEN

Organize around AI

As platforms help various parties to interact, we tend to think of network effects from the point of view of platform participants. However, you can also make quantum improvements in firm-internal effectiveness and efficiency by leveraging AI and network effects for organizing.

This chapter focuses on companies' internal resources to show how AI and platforms can drive new types of organizational structures. Maintaining traditional organizational design leads to sub-optimal results in value creation. Many organizations apply new technology but keep the existing, traditional organizational structure. This leads to limited benefits. It's like thinking digitalization is about moving from paper to PDFs and maintaining the same processes to handle documents. Indeed, companies 'making extensive changes to many processes' during AI implementation gain more. According to a BCG study, these companies were five times more likely to get significant financial benefits from the effort than companies that only made 'small changes to a few processes' (Ransbotham *et al*, 2020).

Humans often retrofit new technology to old processes rather than leverage its potential to create improved ways of working. For example, a classic study in manufacturing companies found employees created various workarounds to avoid changing their routines despite the advanced technology (Tyre and Orlikowski, 1994). The new technologies would have enabled them to automate various activities. However, instead of learning how to use the automation, they created workarounds to continue performing the activities manually with the automation technology. Thus, the latest automation technology did not speed up their actions. The company eventually lowered expectations regarding the potential of the newest technology. The company did not reach the benefits its leaders expected. Still, instead of improving the work routines to achieve the gains, they dropped the expectations.

Research on AI-adoption suggests a similar pattern (eg Murray, Rhymer and Sirmon, 2021) and our practical experience confirm that these kinds of reactions are common. For example, despite the widespread use of collaboration software like Dropbox, Microsoft Teams and Google Docs, many people still hold on to their routines. They download files to their hard-drive and send them back via email, creating version management problems and other inefficiencies that the software is meant to overcome. You need to be careful this kind of 'workarounds to avoid productive use of technology' will not happen to your AI implementation.

To reach benefits from AI use, you need to think about how AI enables alternative ways to organize. And alternative ways of organizing help getting ten-fold benefits from new technology. Think about how AI enables dynamic task allocation, talent matching and the creation of optimal teams.

But the change won't happen overnight. Your employees might not trust AI's decision. Therefore, it might help to start by allowing AI to make recommendations only and increase AI autonomy step by step.

For companies with significant physical infrastructure, it's helpful to free yourself from physical constraints with digital twins. These are digital replicas of your company's infrastructure that offer you the flexibility to try AI models in a simulated environment without the need to test them in the physical world. Hence, you can simulate things faster and test your AI in a safe environment.

We will show three ways AI can empower your organization to tap into AI's transformational power:

- Replace formal hierarchy with AI
- Learn to work with AI step by step
- Transcend physical constraints in development with digital twins

Replace formal hierarchy with AI

Traditional organization structures have been developed to compensate for human-bounded rationality. Humans can consider only a few alternatives and a limited amount of information when making decisions. Traditional organizational structures, therefore, include hierarchy and various sub-units. Each sub-unit has its own goals to ensure that the units people can focus their limited thinking capacity on reach their target. Unfortunately, this focus also causes them to optimize short-term local processes. This happens at the expense of organization-wide end-to-end processes being carried out over more extended time periods.

Artificial intelligence transcends human-bounded rationality. It, therefore, enables organizations to structure their tasks and processes more effectively.

From an organizational point of view, the most important feature of AI is that it can see everything at once in an organization all the time. Once an organization measures its relevant activities and connects the data to a central AI, the AI maintains a continuous picture of everything occurring in the organization. This enables the AI to predict how things will proceed and which kinds of subsequent actions lead to the best outcomes.

The ultimate promise of AI-driven organizing is that organizational structures become irrelevant. We no longer need to simplify people's roles and abilities to generic categories such as a regional manager or a software engineer. Instead, for each activity taking place in an organization, the AI can find the best people.

Use these steps to replace formal hierarchy with AI

You can replace formal hierarchy with AI by starting from specific areas, following the six steps below:

1 Allocate tasks dynamically with AI
2 Use AI to match the right expertise with the right task
3 Use AI to create optimal teams
4 Use AI for managing interdependencies
5 Enhance change communication with AI
6 Define boundaries for AI

1. Allocate tasks dynamically with AI

AI's ability to see everything at once, all the time, enables various firms to organize their activities in different ways and connect third parties to their platform dynamically. This is how Uber manages its drivers. No middle manager is telling each driver where they should go, but AI assigns the rides. Uber operates and coordinates thousands of drivers without a middle manager. In contrast, in traditional hierarchies, you might need a middle manager for every ten employees.

AI can also manage task allocation in more complex contexts. Consider refuse collection: traditionally, garbage companies have regular routes that their cars will drive at regular intervals. For example, truck#7 collects garbage from the houses in the South-East part of the city on Mondays, following a pre-determined route. The truck goes to each garbage can on the way, collects what is inside, and then drives to the next can.

The traditional garbage collection process is smooth but contains many inefficiencies. Sometimes the garbage cans are too full, so customer satisfaction is lowered, as people dislike to see garbage outside the can. The collection also gets slower, as the workers need to collect the trash from the ground. Sometimes the cans are relatively empty, meaning that the truck drove there in vain – it could have come only next week and saved valuable working time.

As hundreds of garbage cans are emptied every day, they could optimize the collection more dynamically. The truck could drive only to those locations where the garbage level has reached a critical threshold. In this way, each truck could handle many customers while providing a higher service quality level. And this is what the most intelligent garbage companies, such as Sensoneo, are doing (Sensoneo, 2021).

The intelligent way of organizing garbage collection includes three elements: 1) sensors in garbage cans that measure the amount of garbage in the can, 2) additional information sources such as weather and road-work bulletins, and 3) an AI algorithm that creates a new route for each truck owned by the garbage company every night. Furthermore, such systems can leverage additional Uber-driver-like resources for peak-demand.

The AI algorithm calculates the most optimal way of collecting garbage from the nearly full cans. It creates a route for each car, such that all relevant cans are emptied and each path is as short as possible. The algorithm also considers detours and details caused by road works and weather. Further, when individual locations seem inefficient to be collected by the company's truck, the AI system could create a bid for third-party drivers. They might be people who have pick-up trucks or other suitable vehicles for collecting small amounts of garbage. If a sub-contractor takes the bid, the location is excluded from the company's own trucks' route. If no-one takes the offer, the AI readjusts one truck's route to take care of the location.

In this way, the truck drivers' route is no longer dictated by their manager (and his/her bounded rational planning) and a routine. Instead, they are controlled by an AI algorithm that considers all relevant, up-to-date information to make the best choices. Additionally, the company has more flexibility in resourcing, as it can sub-contract individual locations via its online service.

For your organization, how are tasks being allocated? Do you rely on a routine in which each employee does the same task every day, regardless of the overall situation? Or do you rely on staffers and middle managers who make sense of current needs and employee availability? Would it be possible to automate some of this work with AI?

2. Use AI to match the right expertise with the right task

When an organization needs to perform a task, there are various qualities of an individual that influence whether or not they should conduct the job. These qualities could be skills relevant to the job, the physical location of the person, language skills, interpersonal skills or the other productive activities that the person could perform instead.

Traditionally, a role within an organizational hierarchy is a proxy for task skills and physical location. However, as organizations become more complex, the proxies provided by formal roles become less relevant. This happens because there are far more dimensions to consider in the employee-task fit than what a single role can proxy for. Rather than having each individual categorized under one role, you need to have multiple 'tags' for each person, ie several skills and qualities. And then, you need to select the best fitting person for the task.

For most of modern history, however, it has not been possible to coordinate the actions of dozens of people with multiple tags. It has not been possible because there are many activities continually going on in an organization, and a single person might fit many of the tasks. However, an AI that sees everything at once, all the time, can simulate the most optimal way of dividing the tasks between individuals. AI can calculate how to maximize the organization's overall productivity rather than that of any single mission or individual.

From an individual's point of view, fluid organizing means they receive their daily task allocation from an AI and then perform the work. They might have the same team members and same tasks as yesterday, but they might also have something different. While it requires some change tolerance, individuals are likely to enjoy working this way because they get to put their skills to the best use. Besides, the AI could also optimize for interpersonal fit when forming teams.

CASE STUDY   Using AI to match patients with healthcare providers

In various domains, finding the right expert for the task is often a significant challenge. Consider, for example, when going to a doctor. You have a specific knee problem and would like to see a doctor who has a lot of experience in such issues. However, as you have never had the same problem before, you cannot evaluate a potential doctor's suitability for your problem. And when you check their website, they list their areas of expertise quite vaguely.

Some healthcare platforms use an alternative solution, developed by Futurice, a European software company, for this problem (aito.ai, 2018). Rather than relying on the key words a doctor has listed in their profile as their areas of expertise, the platform uses AI to determine the doctor's true expertise. The AI reads relevant records about the doctor's prior actions, such as patient records, emails and medical publications, to understand what he or she has done. The AI then proposes the doctor whose expertise best fits the patient. (The AI also considers other factors such as location and preferred price). In this way, the platform enables more effective matchmaking by leveraging advanced AI.

The use of the matchmaking AI algorithm is not limited to the transactions between patients and doctors. Instead, a customer can enter the platform with any need related to health and well-being, be it unclear chest pain, swollen lymph node, desire to lose weight or mood elevation. The customer provides a brief description of their needs, and an AI algorithm matches the customer with the most appropriate service provider. For example, back pain (reported with some background information) might lead to the AI matching the patient with a physiotherapist and a furniture company. This would ensure the acute problem's treatment and that the customer's working conditions are improved to prevent future back pains.

Note how AI allows organizing the entire work process in a novel way: the customer/patient is in contact with an online platform. Different service providers have joined the online platform in the background, and the AI has determined their skills and abilities by interpreting textual data about their past activities. The AI then matches the patient with a bundle of service providers and ensures they perform the services in the correct sequence and consistently. The patient/customer gets a holistic service, but there is no human in control of the overall arrangement of the activities. The same company does not even provide the activities, but the AI organizes each service provider to perform their activity at the right time in the right place.

How is your organization matching expertise with tasks? Do you rely on people's titles? For example, is it always that the communications manager works on communication-related matters, regardless of whether or not they have a substantial knowledge of it? Is it still that a customer relations manager works on customer-related topics, irrespective of their understanding of the customer's focal issue, such as a specific technology? Or do you have an internal database of people's skills, which someone perhaps sometimes updates and no-one ever uses? How much more productive could your organization be if AI helped you to identify the person with the most relevant skill-set for the task?

3. Use AI to create optimal teams

Besides matching a single individual with a specific task, AI can help you form optimal teams. Futurice uses an algorithm called BubbleBurster to formulate new teams for particular tasks (Asikainen, 2020). When a client sends a request, the algorithm finds the most suitable experts for the task. The team might include, for example, a person with relevant industry expertise, a person with a prior relationship with the client and a person with relevant content expertise. Together, these people can generate far more value for the client than any other potential combination of individuals from the several hundred members of Futurice's international staff. And this is achieved by letting AI rather than a manager determine who should work on the client engagement.

The BubbleBurster breaks silos in the organizational structures that have been caused by human-bounded rationality. Traditionally, when you had several hundred employees, no-one could know everyone and their skills. Hence, you created a hierarchy. You appointed five vice presidents who each supervised seven middle managers, each of whom had around 10 team members. This hierarchy was needed because a single human can monitor the work of about ten people with sufficient rigour.

A hierarchy was effective because it is often possible to divide people along with functions or another dimension. For example, radio engineers were under one VP, software engineers under another, marketing people under a third one and so on. Alternatively, you could have divided your staff according to geographical region. In any case, it was possible to create units that were relatively independent of one another and let the team do most of the work inside the unit.

However, an unintended side effect of hierarchy and task division is the formation of silos. As each unit mainly attends to matters related to the unit, they rarely consider what is going on in the other units. They, therefore, seldom get exposed to the expertise of the other unit's members. Hence, they often end up reinventing the wheel in their own unit or failing to leverage the other unit's in-house expertise for critical tasks.

With AI-enabled organizing, the need for nearly independent units is reduced as AI can manage everything simultaneously and maintain awareness of everyone's activities and expertise. In a fully AI-enabled organization, organization members do not have a formal position. Rather, they are 'located' in a single pool of managers and employees. AI always selects the most suitable individuals from the pool for each task the organization is to perform. AI can do this because it has awareness of each individual's skills, network, location, availability, opportunity cost and other relevant attributes as well as the task requirements.

A task performed by such a team can also produce new tasks for the organization: for example, a first team might recognize several market opportunities and define a new task to investigate those market opportunities more thoroughly. AI would then select a set of individuals from the pool for handling the second task, and so on. The individuals selected for the second task might or might not be the same as those who performed the first task – it would depend on their suitability for the task. In this way, each individual would always be performing those tasks that most benefit the organization. In the most advanced (perhaps utopian) vision, even strategy formulation and other leadership duties typically performed by the executive team could be handled in this dynamic manner.

An initial step in the direction of hierarchy- and role-free, AI-enabled organizing is the use of tools such as the BubbleBurster that help you break the silos one task or meeting at a time. You can also create several 'small pools' such that there are some tasks for which the most suitable employees are chosen in the manner described above. For example, you might have a pool of employees for a given geographical region or customer segment. Then, for each task in that region or segment, AI would select an optimal team from the pool allocated for it.

4. Use AI for managing interdependencies

AI-enabled fluid organizing allows for coordinating the interdependencies between tasks. Each individual has specific outputs they must deliver at a particular point in time. These outputs function as inputs for the next task, just like physical products move forward in an assembly line. Traditionally, the coordination between tasks has been a reason for not changing processes often. However, with advanced AI solutions, more dynamic coordination is possible. Even if the chain of tasks frequently changes, AI can model each task, input, output and temporal sequence.

To illustrate, consider an intelligent construction site where data is being recorded real time on each sub-task's progress. In construction projects, various tasks are interrelated. You cannot start the next task before a previous task has been finished. For example, cement needs to dry before electricity work can be started. There is real-time data on the drying of the cement in an advanced construction site. Depending on weather and other factors, it can take between four and eight weeks. This real-time data is used to coordinate between the other activities. In a first-level solution, the electrician is scheduled to arrive only when the cement has dried, based on the first week's data predictions.

In an evermore advanced solution, the AI proposes additional measures, such as heating and ventilation, to influence the cement's drying. This ensures the project remains on schedule if such interventions generate fewer costs than the delays caused by the slowly drying cement and delayed interdependent works. In other words, AI is monitoring how things evolve and recommends corrective actions that consider all relevant consequences.

Contrast the intelligent operation with the traditional approach where human-bounded rationality limits what project managers can consider. They have a construction plan: a cement worker has been scheduled to arrive on week #4, and based on a typical estimate, the electrician on week #7. They base these estimates on the planner's experience and judgement. However, these reflect but do not fully consider the effect of the construction site's conditions on the cement's drying speed. They cannot fully take into account the details associated with each task, because a construction project has hundreds of tasks. No human can develop deep expertise on each task and their potential interdependencies.

As the project proceeds, the cement worker arrives on week #4 and installs the cement, and leaves the construction site. Then the cement starts drying and workers are busy with various other tasks. On week #7, the electrician arrives. They check the cement, notice that it is still not dry enough and decide to come back a week later. They mention this to the construction manager, who is annoyed but understands that there is no other choice.

The construction manager then informs the person in charge of installing decorative panels on top of the electricity work that the electricity work is delayed. They don't mind as they were scheduled to come only after two more weeks in any case and also have several other active projects. They never even consider informing the team in charge of the next tasks that the decoration work will be delayed.

In this example, the effects of bounded rationality on organizing are visible: each person is considering only their own task and its implications on the following task. However, no-one is aware of the overall set of activities and their various interdependencies. The project manager considers the first set of implications when they inform the person in charge of decorative panels. However, they do not consider the subsequent implications, ie the delays caused to the later work stages.

Even more importantly, during the first week, when the cement is not drying as fast as it should be, the construction manager is not reacting. They are not monitoring the cement's drying because they are engaged in dozens of other tasks that occur in the construction site at the same time. They have no mental capacity for monitoring it, and the implications would be vague to them as they have limited expertise on the cement drying process. They also lack a complete understanding of the cost of the delays caused by the slowly drying cement, as they do not realize all implications on interdependent tasks.

Hence, rather than predicting how the cement drying process will influence overall project progress and cost, the construction manager assumes the problem away. They do not maintain constant awareness of the cement's dryness or start corrective actions to speed up the drying. They let things happen and then react when the problems have escalated to be large enough for everyone to notice.

The situation is further complicated because various parallel activities are going on in each construction site. The construction manager is monitoring the drying of the cement and the progress of various other activities. Each of these activities might have some implications for various other activities that again have implications for other activities. With human-bounded rationality, it is not possible to see all these connections all the time. It is also impossible to update one's mental prediction of how things will proceed and where interventions would be needed.

In contrast, an advanced AI solution, combined with active censors on the site, can continuously simulate each sub-task's progress and model the implications for the interdependent tasks. AI can also identify where interventions would provide the most value and then dedicate additional resources to make them.

In this way, while humans are boundedly rational and can see only a few things at a time, an AI can see everything at once, all the time. And this ubiquitous ability to see enables it to recommend actions that benefit the overall organization and process the most, rather than just optimizing a limited sub-task.

For your organization, what are the most essential end-to-end processes that could benefit from AI-based coordination? Where do you have situations in which the first team's actions cause substantive delays later in the process?

5. Enhance change communication with AI

In addition to concrete choices related to task allocation, staffing and scheduling, AI can augment softer managerial skills. In particular, AI can help customize change communication (Stenius and Vuori, 2018). People's personal characteristics influence their receptivity to change. For example, different national identities or educational backgrounds may lead to differing perceptions of organizational changes. Organizations should therefore customize their change communication to match the target audience.

Traditionally, middle managers customize organizational change communication. They work as a bridge between top managers and employees, communicating concerns upwards in the hierarchy and customizing messages downwards. They know their team members and can therefore emphasize those aspects of the change that most motivate them. Today, however, AI enables organizations to customize their communication automatically to various groups. As AI can know everyone in the organization, it can also understand what they will like.

Analytics help you identify which individual characteristics and attitudes influence people's reactions to change and how. For example, you could make a move from private offices to open offices more pleasant through customized communication. For extroverts, communicate how the arrangement creates new opportunities for interaction. In contrast, for introverts, you should emphasize measures that ensure sufficient possibilities for quiet work. As AI can determine the employees' personality traits, it could choose which message to send to each employee.

You could customize your change communication via something as simple as starting with a video depicting a CEO's speech from the most relevant point for each individual. Every individual in the organization would watch the same video. Still, AI would determine which section of the speech would resonate most with them. Hence, different individuals would get different starting points. Such customizations can range from introducing change management material to more systematic, holistic change strategies that tailor the entire change experience individually.

Organizations already possess various and extensive data on their members. For example, you know their current position, work history, age, gender, education and other characteristics. You could expand this data by collecting data from untapped, novel sources, such as social media platforms or wearable activity trackers (within ethical and legal bounds, of course).

6. Define boundaries for AI

So far, our examples have highlighted the flexibility and dynamic abilities of AI-driven organizing. However, you need to create some boundaries for AI.

To illustrate, in a construction site, having a master schedule is often beneficial. There are some hard deadlines for sub-tasks. For example, it could be decided that the cement must dry within six weeks, even at extra cost, because so many other activities depend on the cement drying.

Hence, the AI solution does not reschedule all the interdependent activities but activates corrective actions to dry the cement on time. And everyone on the construction site knows that getting the cement dry on time is a priority and that they can trust it will be dry as agreed. This makes sure that everyone is ready to start the next phase of work in a synchronized fashion and improves the work's overall efficiency.

Likewise, garbage truck drivers' route focus and length should have some boundary conditions. The drivers are likely to be more effective if they operate in a familiar area, and the company cannot make them overwork too much. This highlights that while AI provides real-time understanding and dynamic readjustments, those activities must occur within what are reasonable boundaries for the humans operating in the system.

Learn to work with AI

Change won't happen overnight. Your employees and yourself have different expectations and assumptions about new technology. Although everybody might agree the change is inevitable in the long term, they might even resist AI and platform business models in the short term. Your challenge is to turn fear into energy, as we discussed in Chapter 1.

For an organization to work, it needs to have clear targets, roles and decision-making rules. The same applies to AI. If AI is in an assisting position, but employees think it should decide, bad things might happen. Or, if members of the organization expect AI to decide, but managers don't trust it and make their own decisions, things might go south.

So, define what you want from AI. Are you seeking advice on different alternatives or automated decisions? Or do you want AI to learn new parameters that influence decisions? You should understand the context where AI is being used and remember that AI learns from new data. And thus, AI can change the way an organization works as it learns more. Each of these steps leads to a different organizational design from a human point of view. The goal is not to automate everything but to design a set-up where AI's potential is matched with the task at hand.

Use these four steps to learn to work with AI

We suggest four steps you can follow to advance AI in your organization (see also Murray *et al*, 2021). Don't automate everything from the start. Progress systematically and apply the learning loop we discussed in Chapter 4.

Four steps for how to learn to work with AI:

1 Allow AI to make recommendations, but let humans decide

2 Allow AI to make automated decisions based on pre-determined criteria

3 Use AI to create new criteria for a human to decide

4 Allow AI to make autonomous decisions based on its learning

---

1. Allow AI to make recommendations, but let humans decide

In this scenario, AI is your best adviser, but it won't decide on your behalf. This scenario is, therefore, a safe first step, as you are learning to work with AI.

AI can analyse tons of data you couldn't go through in your lifetime in a couple of seconds. Based on pre-determined criteria, AI recommends various options that humans can then choose. As humans get to choose, they maintain a sense of control and are likely to enjoy working with AI.

Let's return to our example of AI choosing a team to perform a specific task. In this scenario, based on an approach developed by IBM (IBM, 2018), a human defines parameters that are relevant for the performance of the team. This human reflects what skills the team should have to succeed in its task. He or she relies on experience and intuition to identify the needed characteristics. The parameters could be, for example, that at least one team member should have each of the following attributes:

- Five years of experience in cloud programming.
- Five years of experience in the industry of the client.
- A pre-existing relationship with the client.
- A business degree.
- Fluency in French.
- Located in central Europe.

The human would define these attributes for the AI system. The AI would search for suitable employees throughout the firm's databases and suggest an optimal team. AI could use various approaches for recognizing the needed skills, in addition to formal CV and skill databases, such as the textual analyses we discussed above. The AI might suggest, for example, a three-person team:

- Person 1
  - Experienced cloud programmer from the US.
- Person 2
  - A marketing expert who has worked with the client for over five years;
  - Fluency in French;
  - Located in central Europe.
- Person 3
  - Recently hired MBA from the Singapore office.

Seeing this suggestion, the human could decide whether to accept or reject the AI's proposal. For example, the human might reason that it would be ineffective to have people from three different time zones. Hence, he or she might reject this proposal from the AI (and potentially add a location constraint in the criteria).

If the human rejected the AI's proposal, the AI could then search for an alternative combination. The AI could also be programmed always to suggest, say, three alternatives from which the human could then choose. AI assists in the decision-making but doesn't decide.

In what decisions could you use additional input from AI? Consider the variety of choices made every day in your organization. Which of those choices contain criteria and attributes that could be programmed for AI? Should you contact a vendor to create an AI system for you to augment these decisions?

2. Allow AI to make automated decisions based on pre-determined criteria

In this scenario, a human decides the criteria for a decision. Based on those, AI can make an automatic decision. To continue our team selection example, a human would define the criteria used for selecting the team, and AI would automatically determine the team composition and schedule the team for work.

By adopting this approach, you gain efficiency. You can use this approach once people have learned to trust the AI's recommendations in the first step. After you notice that you or your team has accepted the last 20 recommendations from AI, you could conclude that it's time to let the AI work autonomously.

A challenge in this approach is that the set of criteria created by the human might be incomplete. For example, maybe there is a personal conflict between two employees. Therefore, they should not be included in the same team. However, if not listed as a criterion, the AI would not consider this conflict, even if everyone in the company knew about the conflict. It would help if you, therefore, thought also how you could maximize the AI's learning.

3. Use AI to create new criteria for a human to decide

AI could observe teams' outcomes at specific tasks, analyse why they fail or succeed and discover new criteria for selecting the teams. These criteria could be understandable by humans but could also be very complex and hard to explain.

For example, when recommending an optimal team, AI would learn the team members' optimal attributes instead of relying on the human definition. AI could do this by analysing the performance of (relevant) past projects and comparing them to project member attributes, the project's goal and various other characteristics related to the project. Essential here is that instead of relying on human intuition and pre-established ideas of what makes an excellent team, the AI would learn which attributes predict team performance. Through such an approach, Google discovered how psychological safety is one of the key factors contributing to team performance (Duhigg, 2016; re:Work, nd).

Some other characteristics recognized by AI could involve those that are intuitive for humans, such as client industry and country. Also, they could include others that are less intuitive, such as the season (summer, autumn, winter, spring) or the height of project team members.

If AI has access to project conversation data, it could infer team characteristics from it. Without defining the criteria, it could conclude, for example, that teams using language that leads to psychological safety perform better than others.

Once AI had identified the relevant attributes, it would search for employees that fit the characteristics. After recognizing them, it would suggest one or a few alternatives for the humans to decide. The human would then make a choice.

A challenge in using 'AI to create the criteria but letting humans decide' is that the human may not understand why the AI is suggesting the teams it is suggesting. The options might seem counter-intuitive or wrong for the human.

It is difficult for humans to act on recommendations that do not make sense to them. However, sometimes it is beneficial to do so. For example, a top-notch hedge fund, Renaissance, uses AI extensively and sometimes its employees do not understand the AI's recommendations. Still, they profit by trading securities based on non-intuitive anomalies that were detected by machine learning but are hard to explain (Peng, 2020).

Hence, this approach requires courage and trust toward the AI from the decision-maker.

To reduce the need to trust AI blindly, you can invest in explainable AI. This refers to modules that make AI's recommendations more understandable for people. For one, where feasible, you should select algorithms that contain explicit logic for their choices. In addition, it's worth creating an explanation interface that provides the rationale for the user. Several new techniques for making AI more explainable are being developed and you should keep track of the most advanced solutions (eg DARPA, 2021; IBM, 2021). As an executive, you need to recognize that it might be worth the additional investment.

4. Allow AI to make autonomous decisions based on its learning

As the last step, you let AI learn and make autonomous decisions. For example, AI could observe the teams' outcomes at specific tasks and detect why they fail or succeed. It would adjust its criteria accordingly for selecting the teams based on this. It would then automatically assign team members for the tasks that followed.

This approach has at least two substantial benefits: efficiency and freedom from human bias. You gain efficiency as there is no need to have a human make sense of the alternatives or fight political battles. You are free from human discrimination, as there is no human who would override the AI's recommendation. In addition, as the AI is learning from the performance data, it is likely to develop a superior understanding of factors influencing team success. It can therefore create stronger teams than humans could.

The downsides of this approach relate to the loss of human visibility and control. The AI likely learns beneficial patterns and makes optimal decisions. However, when there is a situation that qualitatively differs from the past, AI might make wrong recommendations while people would see the obvious implications.

In addition, as more thinking responsibility and control are given to the AI, there are fewer opportunities for humans in your organization to grow into managerial roles. Without AI, lower-level managers learn the business logic by making repeated decisions. But when those decisions are fully automated, those managers lose their chance to practise.

However, the benefits often outweigh the risks and it is useful to start building this approach. You could start by automating simple decisions. What decisions could you already automate to a learning AI? Once you gain familiarity and begin trusting the AI, what would be the next set of automated decisions handed to a learning AI?

Transcend physical constraints in development with digital twins

Engineers in the Nestlé factory in Juuka had just loaded new data into a system. A week's production round was finished a few seconds later. An engineer reviewed the results and adjusted production parameters based on the simulation results. An accurate digital model, a digital twin built by Siemens, made this possible. Digital twins enable the fast simulation of real-life events such as production.

The real world is hard to manage. Imagine a paper factory with a complex control system. If engineers want to test a new algorithm to improve the process, it takes several weeks, if not months, to perform the tests. Also, there is a risk that something doesn't work or that a new process will lead to failure.

Therefore, companies need digital twins. A digital twin is a digital presentation of real-life processes, systems, physical assets and operating behaviours. People often associate digital twins with factories and the manufacturing industry. However, a digital twin can model anything in real life, even a person. Hence, companies can use digital twins for many purposes.

With a digital twin, you can genuinely organize around AI. If you model your platform as a digital twin, new possibilities open up. For example, you can produce data through simulation to train your AI models.

Think about food delivery services like Uber Eats. As discussed in Chapter 4, 'Create a learning loop', Uber Eats models and predicts the preparation time for the food to schedule the right pickup time. Furthermore, it forecasts the delivery time of the prepared meal. Every new order improves the system by producing more data. As a result, it develops a more accurate digital twin of the meal preparation and delivery process based on real-world data. Soon it could run simulations to test a new AI model for route optimization without the need to deliver actual meals. Once the algorithm is ready, it would be deployed into production. Developers could also add human-in-the-loop, visualizing the delivery process on a map to observe courier behaviour to improve it.

In other words, you can transcend physical constraints in development with digital twins. Let's look at how to get started.

Build digital twins through these four steps

Follow these four steps to leverage digital twins in your organization.

Four steps to transcend physical constraints with digital twins:

1 Introduce digital twin thinking into your organization
2 Build a digital twin of your platform
3 Connect AI and digital twins
4 Reimagine your business with AI and digital twins

1. Introduce digital twin thinking into your organization

Don't rush to develop digital twins without considering your business targets. Once you have clarity on your goals, it's easier to think about utilizing digital twins. Ask your organization what is limiting your development speed. Are there machines or processes that you could model with digital twins? Could you make better operational decisions by creating a digital twin and use it to learn and predict faster?

Train your team to understand the digital twin concept and the opportunities it offers. What if you were free from the physical constraints of machines, processes and humans? In that case, what AI-based simulations and tools could you use to improve your organization?

In Chapter 4, we described Finnair's AI system to predict flight congestion. After delays occur, ground personnel needs to take action to sort things out. But it's hard to train personnel in a real-life situation. Therefore, Finnair developed a digital twin to train its ground personnel to speed up delayed flights. The digital twin is a virtual 3D replica of the airport and planes. Personnel can be trained on missions like how to speed up fuelling an aircraft, schedule additional cleaning crew or mount other stairs for faster departure and boarding of passengers (Zoan, nd).

2. Build a digital twin of your platform

To build a digital twin, you need to start by identifying and modelling the system's components. For example, to create a factory's digital twin, you can model individual components such as pumps and valves with a mechanical and physical model. You can model their wear and tear with historical data. On top of a mechanical model, you can add electronics and management software. You can then connect products into a complete system-level model. You can also model process flows with physical or data models.

To bring the digital twin into life, you need real-time data that you can capture from the real-life system through sensors. Now you have created a replica of the real system to operate and observe even in a remote location. Engineers can plan, simulate, predict and optimize production in a matter of minutes. And when something goes wrong in the real world, you can study the digital twin to figure out what caused the faulty condition.

Similar principles apply if you create a digital twin of, for example, your employees, like Uber Eats and many other companies are doing. You create a physical model which includes, for example, the map of the focal city and the estimated speed of different delivery methods (pedestrian, car or bicycle). The censors you use are the employees' smartphones that transmit location data and other parameters.

For knowledge workers, the digital twin used by companies is often something as simple as an Excel sheet. The excel lists, for example, the person's availability (ie current task load and pending tasks assigned to the person), their skills and their typical speed (eg faster than average, average, slower than average). These parameters enable companies to model alternative ways of allocating current and pending tasks to different employees and see which allocation pattern would reach the outcomes fastest.

And remember, the digital twin does not need to be complete. It just needs to be good enough to model the problem you are trying to solve. So, you can start with a simple system and improve it step by step.

3. Connect AI and digital twins

Part of your digital twin is AI models you have developed for your platform. Now you can test them much faster without the need to run them in a real environment. You can also produce new data through simulations in the digital twin to train your AI system. Conversely, AI is used to model the digital twin's dynamic behaviour.

For example, engineers would like a more efficient pump to increase the throughput of the factory. It's easy in a digital twin; just add the new model, and the rest of the system adjusts its operations. With AI, you can analyse the change and identify bottlenecks. Maybe some other parts of the system need to be upgraded, too. Increased throughput could put some other parts of the system under pressure and cause faster wear. AI could predict this failure.

Digital twins can unlock more advanced forms of AI. As we explained in Chapter 4, most machine learning today is supervised learning, where the model learns from labelled examples. We described reinforcement learning, where the model learns from rewards when taking actions. You can apply reinforcement learning with digital twins without fearing that your factory could break down when testing novel algorithms. Training reinforcement learning requires an enormous number of repetitions. With digital twins, this is not a problem.

AI can benefit you also when you have created digital twins of your employees. AI can learn patterns influencing their task completion time and quality and, therefore, improve the suggestions it makes of how to allocate the tasks. For example, suppose AI learns that a particular neighbourhood has a high probability of delays. AI can take this into account when allocating new orders to a courier serving that district. AI could also model interdependencies between tasks, like modern time management applications, and assign additional knowledge workers to bottleneck tasks.

4. Reimagine your business with AI and digital twins

Hilti has already transformed itself from a product company to a solutions and platform business. Its target is to increase the productivity of construction sites. Hilti is building digital twins of construction sites using building information modelling (BIM). BIM is a process for creating and managing information on a construction project across the project lifecycle. As a result, it produces a digital description of every aspect of the built asset, ie a digital twin.

In 2021, Hilti is taking this to the next level. It started a pilot with Boston Dynamic and Trimble to use construction robots (Trimble, 2019). The millimetre accurate digital twin based on BIM models allows the use of robots for operating machinery, for example, nail guns.

With an integrated 360 degree camera and site documentation, software robots like Boston Dynamics Spot can capture data from the construction site (Boston Dynamics, 2020). They can therefore update a digital twin of the status of the worksite. This can be used, for example, to reschedule activities with AI, as we described earlier in this chapter.

And each site will produce data that adds value to other construction sites. This happens through more advanced AI models to improve scheduling of the tasks at the construction sites and through more accurate digital twins. Network effect and learning loop in action in an industry where you might not have thought it existed. As a result, companies like Hilti have become intelligent platforms.

Key takeaways for your organization

To conclude, we have outlined different ways of deploying AI in your organization. There is no right or wrong, as it depends on the context. Many people think the ultimate goal is to automate everything. That might not be desirable or sometimes not even allowed from a legal point of view. AI might not know the context of the decision, and you thus still need a human input. The good news is that as a human, you can decide the level of input you will have when planning how to organize your company for AI.

Use AI to replace formal hierarchy

- Could you use AI for allocating tasks to the right employees and experts?
- What would get better if you used AI to coordinate between various tasks?
- How would it look if you used AI to create optimal teams?
- Would it be possible to customize change communication with AI in your organization?

Learn to work with AI

- Where might you use AI to augment decision-making?
- In which decisions could you let AI learn from the data and define new decision criteria?
- What decisions could you fully automate with an autonomously learning AI?

Build a digital twin

- Do people in your organization see the value of having digital twins?
- Do you have machines, processes or people that could be modelled with digital twins?
- What other AI-based simulations and tools could you use to improve your organization?

Conclusion

*Living the seven steps of intelligent platforms
to transform your business*

As we described in the introduction, Nokia's phone business did not survive the platform era. But Nokia's story did not end there. In 2012, Nokia's board started turning *fear into energy* in the company by managing top managers' emotions. Nokia's leaders ultimately accepted they should let go of the diminishing phone business. They *created the unexpected* by generating various strategic options and analysing them thoroughly. Nokia transformed into a networks company that is currently driving the development of 5G networks that leverage AI and enable various platforms and ecosystems. They connect humans with self-driving cars, complex factories and construction sites and space programmes. (Nokia's transformation is detailed further in Vuori and Huy, 2018, 2021.)

During its renewal journey, Nokia has learned to apply the other steps described in this book through trial and error. To expand the networks business, Nokia acquired Alcatel-Lucent in 2015. The merged organization initially became complex and created lots of friction within Nokia and with its customers. Nokia has therefore systematically sought to *reduce friction* in its operations, including radically simplifying its organizational structure and processes in 2021. It is also simplifying and *focusing its offering* to those that add most value to its customers and moving away from other businesses, as presented by the new CEO appointed in 2021.

In parallel, Nokia has developed APIs and integrated AI evermore comprehensively into its operations. Applying the idea of *algorithmic handshakes*, Nokia's APIs help third parties develop solutions in all Nokia's key areas: networks, IoT, health products, virtual reality and cloud infrastructure. It has launched AI based tools for optimization of 5G networks and other areas to create *learning loops* (O'Halloran, 2020).

The company encouraged all its members, from the board to typical employees, to learn AI (Siilasmaa, 2018) and it has acquired AI technologies (Olson, 2017). The company is also introducing several AI tools to boost productivity and learning and increase coordination in the organization (Kotorchevikj, 2020). Ultimately, these actions are likely to enable Nokia to move away from its traditional hierarchy and become *organized around AI*.

Nokia's spirit and learning in other companies

While Nokia's story continues in areas other than smartphones, Nokia leaders from the smartphone era, including Tero, learned from its early efforts in the platform game. They have taken these lessons to several other companies, creating new intelligent platforms. Their efforts illustrate how the seven steps outlined in this book can help you create a new intelligent platform or transform your company into one.

Goldman Sachs

Tero hired Marco Argenti to run Nokia's developer ecosystem and app store in 2006. After Nokia, he became co-chief information officer and member of the management committee of Goldman Sachs. Another person from Tero's ex Nokia team, Atte Lahtiranta, is now the chief technology officer of Goldman Sachs. Atte's focus is to attract developers to work with the firm (Campbell and DeFrancesco, 2019). Marco and Atte are transforming the banking giant into an intelligent platform. They have turned the fear for fintech challengers into energy that is driving change.

In particular, the company is achieving this by creating a financial cloud. We described Amazon cloud services AWS's birth in Chapter 5, as Amazon management realized they had built an infrastructure that others could use. The same is happening now at Goldman Sachs. It removes friction for accessing services like the trading and risks analytics platform Goldman Sachs has built for internal use (Butcher, 2020). It targets becoming a 'banking-as-a-service' partner to companies like Apple, Stripe, Amazon and Walmart. Hence, they can embed banking products and services in their offering and leave the heavy lifting to Goldman Sachs (Crosman, 2021).

Varjo

A group of Nokia technology veterans founded Varjo in 2016, a next-generation mixed-reality platform focused on enterprise creative design. Since 2020, the company has been led by Timo Toikkanen, once the leader of Nokia's mobile phones business. Instead of trying to serve all types of customers, Varjo chose a sharp focus, making the best possible mixed-reality systems for the enterprise setting. Their product's quality has engaged large companies like Boeing, Volvo and Autodesk as their customers and partners. Indeed, the partnerships may generate the next steps in their story, perhaps enabling them to transcend industry boundaries.

Thomson Reuters

Taneli Ruda worked at the Nokia strategy team before moving to Thomson Reuters. As a head of strategy, he helps the company create AI-enabled learning loops powering the intelligent legal research service Westlaw Edge.

KONE

Matti Alahuhta was in Nokia's executive team until 2005. He then became the CEO of KONE, whose headquarters were located only a few hundred metres from Nokia's, on the Baltic Sea's beautiful shore. During his tenure, KONE envisioned managing people flows, which requires managing buildings and broader ecosystems of mobility solutions instead of just manufacturing and selling elevators and escalators.

In particular, KONE initiated the development of APIs that now enable other companies to join KONE's platform with an algorithmic handshake. While Nokia's headquarters moved away from the prime location after Microsoft acquired Nokia's phone business in 2014, KONE's tower is still standing tall.

Google

Photographer and mountaineer Hans Peter Brondmo is wrangling robots at Google in X, the moonshot factory, creating the unexpected. He leads the everyday robot project that develops a general purpose learning robot that can operate autonomously in unstructured environments (X, 2021). Before Google, he worked at HERE, Nokia's mapping unit, where he co-led a new product innovation business unit.

Hilti Group

Matias Järnefelt used to work with Nokia's corporate strategy team. He moved to Hilti Group and is Managing Director, Northern Europe and Great Britain. Hilti illustrates the new way of thinking about your strategy. It transcends industry boundaries. It has transformed itself from a manufacturer of power tools to an intelligent platform improving productivity for building sites as described in Chapter 7. It's creating network effects. It creates a learning loop and uses human insights to expand into new areas.

Betolar

In his book *How to Avoid a Climate Disaster*, Bill Gates calls for urgent solutions to replace cement to solve the climate crisis (Gates, 2021). This also brought former Nokia CEO Olli-Pekka Kallasvuo and Tero to work together again. They leverage platform strategy into the construction and building industry based on learnings from Nokia and other work. Betolar is a start-up with new innovative material technology, Geoprime. It replaces cement-based concrete, responsible for 8 per cent of the world's carbon emissions (Rodgers, 2018), resulting in 80 per cent fewer carbon emissions. Additionally, it reduces the use of natural resources by reusing industrial side streams, increasing biodiversity.

Betolar is a platform company that optimizes its product with the help of AI. It started with a focus on one segment, paving products. It removes friction in accessing climate-friendly products by enabling the use of current production facilities. Its AI-based learning loop optimizes production. Although it's still focused on getting the business up and running, it already envisions the unexpected by leveraging its technology to new verticals like stabilization and mining.

Could it be different? What is your 'Spotify moment'?

Looking back, it's tempting to ask if things could have gone otherwise for Nokia's phone business. Reflecting on this question is not only entertaining, it can also make you think if you are facing choice points that make a difference for your business.

For Nokia and Tero, one such choice point was a meeting with the founder of Spotify, Daniel Ek, in Stockholm around 2008. Daniel proposed a partnership, which Nokia rejected. Nokia was developing digital downloads to fight Apple and missed the streaming trend. Now Spotify is a global platform and continues to create the unexpected. Suppose Nokia had joined forces with Spotify and focused on music streaming as the spearhead service? In that case, it might have built the critical mass and engagement for its platform.

What are the choices you are making today that might determine if your firm will become a successful platform or a forgotten dinosaur? If you look back at the chapters, you may recognize several places where your choices might be drifting in the wrong direction:

1 Are you holding on to the past due to fear of the novel?
2 Are you creating friction where you should be removing it?
3 Are your efforts too fragmented where they should be focused to generate world-class value and fans?
4 Is your company's learning still based mainly on human intuition? Are you bypassing the chance to learn faster with AI-enabled learning loops?
5 Are you still relying only on human handshakes and not collaborating via APIs?
6 Are you stuck with your current business model and industry instead of seeking to create the unexpected and transcend industry boundaries?
7 Are you adding formal hierarchy and rigid processes instead of organizing work more effectively around AI and with platforms?

Did you meet your 'Spotify' today, did you miss a trend, did you overlook a business opportunity? The impact of intelligent platforms continues to rise. They touch more and more industries. They are the primary way to create value. Make sure to educate yourself and your team about new possibilities and mechanisms on how to create value in the era of AI and platforms. This way, when you face your 'Spotify moment', you'll know what to do.

Timo and Tero continue to research and teach new insights on platform strategy at Aalto University. You can read more from their website www.intelligentplatforms.ai (archived at https://perma.cc/U4QG-5A6P).

References

Introduction

Alipay (2020) Alipay Announces Three-Year Plan to Support the Digital
Transformation of 40 Million Service Providers in China, Alipay [Press Release],
10 March, https://www.businesswire.com/news/home/20200309005906/en/
(archived at https://perma.cc/Q3LD-Z6WS)

KONE (2019) The secret is in the rope, KONE [Press Release], 22 October,
https://www.kone.com/en/news-and-insights/stories/the-secret-is-in-the-rope.aspx
(archived at https://perma.cc/M58H-59MG)

Ojanperä, T and Vuori, T O. (2020) 5 steps how Ant Financial built a $200 billion
platform business, intelligentplatforms.ai, 16 August, https://intelligentplatforms.ai/
5-steps-how-ant-financial-built-a-200-billion-platform-business/ (archived at
https://perma.cc/KL3D-LLPQ)

Siilasmaa, R (2018) *Transforming NOKIA: The Power of Paranoid Optimism to Lead
Through Colossal Change*, McGraw Hill Education, New York

Thomson Reuters (2020) What Thomson Reuters is doing with AI to help customers
[Blog], 20 July, https://tax.thomsonreuters.com/blog/what-thomson-reuters-is-doing-
with-ai-to-help-customers/ (archived at https://perma.cc/UBZ3-35VE)

Vuori, T O. and Huy, Q N (2016a) Distributed Attention and Shared Emotions in the
Innovation Process: How Nokia Lost the Smartphone Battle, *Administrative Science
Quarterly*, **61** (1), pp 9–52

Vuori, T O. and Huy, Q N (2016b) Mental Models and Affective Influence in Inter-
organizational collaboration for new technology, Best Paper Proceedings of the
76th Annual Meeting of the Academy of Management, https://doi.org/10.5465/
ambpp.2016.145 (archived at https://perma.cc/4DT3-G2NC)

Vuori, T O. and Huy, Q N (2018) How Nokia Embraced the Emotional Side of
Strategy, Harvard Business Review (digital article), hbr.org/2018/05/how-nokia-
embraced-the-emotional-side-of-strategy (archived at https://perma.cc/XD36-Q56M)

Chapter 1

Eichenwald, K (2012) Microsoft's Lost Decade, *Vanity Fair*, 24 July,
https://www.vanityfair.com/news/business/2012/08/microsoft-lost-mojo-steve-
ballmer (archived at https://perma.cc/4RGH-JGRZ)

Forbes (2007) Nokia's Kallasvuo Puts Brave Face On IPhone, 12 February, https://www.forbes.com/2007/02/12/nokia-kallasvuo-iphone-faces-cx_cn_0212autofacescan01.html?sh=23f828d0addb (archived at https://perma.cc/GUP4-EGSF)

Forbes (2019) The Power Of Open Source AI. Interview with Sri Ambati, CEO and Founder of H2O.ai, FORBES INSIGHTS, 22 May, https://www.forbes.com/sites/insights-intelai/2019/05/22/the-power-of-open-source-ai/?sh=18b948156300 (archived at https://perma.cc/45NY-HPQC)

Freitag, M (2020) Uber macht Daimler und BMW ein fast unmoralisches Angebot, Manager Magazin, 21 October, https://www.manager-magazin.de/unternehmen/freenow-uber-bietet-daimler-und-bmw-mehr-als-eine-milliarde-a-00000000-0002-0001-0000-000173605126 (archived at https://perma.cc/5GLM-Q5Z6)

Gilbert, C G (2005) Unbundling the structure of inertia: Resource versus routine rigidity, *Academy of Management Journal*, 48 (5), pp 741–63

Hallen, B L and Eisenhardt, K M (2012) Catalyzing strategies and efficient tie formation: how entrepreneurial firms obtain investment ties, *Academy of Management Journal*, 55 (1), pp 35–70

Hastings, R and Mayer, E (2020) *No Rules Rules: Netflix and the Culture of Reinvention*, Random House Large Print, London

Insead (2020) E.ON: Building a New AI-Powered Energy World, INSEAD case study, https://publishing.insead.edu/sites/publishing/files/2020-06/6595-eon-cs-en-0-06-2020-free-copy.pdf (archived at https://perma.cc/VDR6-78EF)

Kelion, L (2020) Why Amazon knows so much about you, BBC News, https://www.bbc.co.uk/news/extra/CLQYZENMBI/amazon-data (archived at https://perma.cc/658N-2J7S)

Lifshitz-Assaf, H (2018) Dismantling knowledge boundaries at NASA: The critical role of professional identity in open innovation, *Administrative Science Quarterly*, 63 (4), pp 746–82

Ozcan, P and Eisenhardt, K M (2009) Origin of alliance portfolios: Entrepreneurs, network strategies, and firm performance, *Academy of Management Journal*, 52 (2), pp 246–79

Reuters (2020) VW CEO says carmaker faces same fate as Nokia without urgent reforms, 16 January, https://www.reuters.com/article/us-volkswagen-strategy-diess-idUSKBN1ZF1OB (archived at https://perma.cc/NBU5-993X)

Rosenberg, M B (2003) *Nonviolent Communication: A Language of Life*, 2nd edn, Puddledancer Press, Encinitas, CA

Santos, F M and Eisenhardt, K M (2009) Constructing markets and shaping boundaries: Entrepreneurial power in nascent fields, *Academy of Management Journal*, 52 (4), pp 643–71

Siilasmaa, R (2015) Here are my Golden Rules for boards, Twitter post, https://twitter.com/rsiilasmaa/status/675437729358979073?lang=en (archived at https://perma.cc/5W3L-C2KE)

Statista (2020) Worldwide gross app revenue of the Apple App Store from 2017 to 2019 (in billion U.S. dollars), https://www.statista.com/statistics/296226/annual-apple-app-store-revenue/ (archived at https://perma.cc/TK76-ZKEX)

Stenius, H and Vuori, T O. (2018) Change Analytics: How Data-Analytics Can Improve Top-Down Change Communication, *Academy of Management Proceedings*, **1**: 12326

Virta (2020) Virta named Europe's fastest-growing EV charging service provider [Press Release], https://www.virta.global/news/fastest-growing-electric-vehicle-charging-service-provider-in-europe (archived at https://perma.cc/K25A-2FHY)

Vuori, T O. and Huy, Q N (2016a) Distributed Attention and Shared Emotions in the Innovation Process How Nokia Lost the Smartphone Battle, *Administrative Science Quarterly*, **61** (1), pp 9–52, https://journals.sagepub.com/doi/abs/10.1177/0001839215606951 (archived at https://perma.cc/GV8J-DKB8)

Vuori, T O. and Huy, Q N (2016b) Mental models and Affective Influence in Inter-organizational collaboration for new technology, Best Paper Proceedings of the Academy of Management, Academy of Management Annual Meeting, 2016

Vuori, T O. and Huy, Q N (2021) Regulating Top Managers' Emotions during Strategy Making, Nokia's Distributed Approach Enabling Radical Change from Mobile Phones to Networks in 2007–2013, *Academy of Management Journal*, in press, available at: https://journals.aom.org/doi/10.5465/amj.2019.0865?ai=vctv&ui=3os1&af=H (archived at https://perma.cc/W8WF-5MUU) (online ahead of print)

YLE (2017) OP:n Karhinen: Automaatio vie noin 30 prosenttia työpaikoista – 'Mitä näille ihmisille tehdään?', https://yle.fi/uutiset/3-9518250 (archived at https://perma.cc/TZB7-M33S)

Chapter 2

Hilti, Careers, [Website], https://careers.us.hilti.com/en-us/lets-build-future-code-1 (archived at https://perma.cc/C4UC-983F)

Katzmaier, D (2016) With a bullet to the head from Samsung, 3D TV is now deader than ever, CNET, 1 March, https://www.cnet.com/news/3d-tv-is-now-more-dead-than-ever/ (archived at https://perma.cc/64QH-6D7S)

Laukia, L (2018) *Evolution of digital platforms – Introduction and reinforcement of platform elements: A case study*, Master's thesis, Aalto University, Finland

Leinonen, K (2020) *Evolution of platform companies: A cross-case study*, Master's thesis, Aalto University, Finland

Mohn, C (2017) *Platform business dynamics: A case study*, Master's thesis, Aalto University, Finland

Morris, D (2016) Today's Cars Are Parked 95% of the Time, Fortune, 13 March, https://fortune.com/2016/03/13/cars-parked-95-percent-of-time/ (archived at https://perma.cc/9ZMF-GW4J)

Repo, R (2018) *Evolution of platform companies: a longitudinal case study*, Master's thesis, Aalto University, Finland

Rindfleisch, A (2020) Transaction cost theory: past, present and future, *AMS Review*, **10**, pp 85–97, https://doi.org/10.1007/s13162-019-00151-x (archived at https://perma.cc/Q88K-S5AW)

Schmidt, C G and Wagner, S M (2019) Blockchain and supply chain relations: A transaction cost theory perspective, *Journal of Purchasing and Supply Management*, **25** (4), p 100552

Williamson, O E (2017) *Contract, Governance and Transaction Cost Economics*, World Scientific Publishing, Singapore

Chapter 3

Anding M (2019) Platform economy meets B2B reality: Why your platform strategy may fail, LinkedIn, 25 February, https://www.linkedin.com/pulse/platform-economy-meets-b2b-reality-why-your-strategy-may-anding/ (archived at https://perma.cc/XZ3C-77PR)

Angulo I (2018) Ikea rolls out nationwide assembly services with TaskRabbit, CNBC, 13 March, https://www.cnbc.com/2018/03/13/ikea-rolls-out-nationwide-assembly-services-with-taskrabbit.html (archived at https://perma.cc/6375-L8PJ)

Anirban D, *et al* (2020) Under the Hood of Uber's Experimentation Platform, Uber [Blog], 28 August, https://eng.uber.com/xp/ (archived at https://perma.cc/Q69H-BDSD)

Astute Solutions (2019) What You Need to Know about Measuring Customer Engagement [Blog], 30 July, https://astutesolutions.com/blog/articles/what-you-need-to-know-about-measuring-customer-engagement (archived at https://perma.cc/U7QY-HQQG)

Davis, S (2014) Tesla, Tesla, Tesla: Building A Power Brand From Scratch, Forbes, 24 February, https://www.forbes.com/sites/scottdavis/2014/02/24/tesla-tesla-tesla-building-a-power-brand-from-scratch/#151b19867e31 (archived at https://perma.cc/R8HM-PHEK)

Gallup (2014) Why Customer Engagement Matters So Much Now, 22 July, https://news.gallup.com/businessjournal/172637/why-customer-engagement-matters.aspx (archived at https://perma.cc/WJ3R-5SC9)

Griffith, E (2019) Peloton Is a Phenomenon. Can It Last?, *The New York Times*, 28 August, https://www.nytimes.com/2019/08/28/technology/peloton-ipo.html (archived at https://perma.cc/KKT9-6GNY)

Huddleston, T (2019) How Peloton exercise bikes became a $4 billion fitness startup with a cult following, CNNC, 12 February, https://www.cnbc.com/2019/02/12/how-peloton-exercise-bikes-and-streaming-gained-a-cult-following.html (archived at https://perma.cc/24AE-AZPD)

Kamat, P and Hogan, C (2019) How Uber Leverages Applied Behavioral Science at Scale, Uber [Blog], 28 January, https://eng.uber.com/applied-behavioral-science-at-scale (archived at https://perma.cc/V683-XZ73)

L, C (2020), 'Peleton Testing More Software / Leaderboard Updates – New Feature Roundup', Pelobuddy, 4 September, https://www.pelobuddy.com/peloton-testing-more-software-leaderboard-updates-new-feature-roundup (archived at https://perma.cc/3639-VP78)

Leach, M (2020), Lenovo Becomes Reseller of Varjo Headsets to Deliver Complete Solution for Virtual and Mixed Reality Applications, Lenovo StoryHub, 26 October, https://news.lenovo.com/pressroom/press-releases/lenovo-becomes-reseller-of-varjo-headsets-to-deliver-complete-solution-for-virtual-and-mixed-reality-applications/ (archived at https://perma.cc/6DSR-YFXN)

Mangalindan J P (2019) Peloton CEO: Sales increased after we raised prices to $2,245 per bike, Yahoo! Finance, 5 June, https://finance.yahoo.com/news/peloton-ceo-says-sales-increased-raised-prices-2245-exercise-bike-132256225.html (archived at https://perma.cc/R2TK-T83W)

McDonald, R M and Eisenhardt, K M (2019) Parallel Play: Startups, Nascent Markets, and Effective Business model Design, *Administrative Science Quarterly*, **65** (2), pp 483–523

Peloton (2019) Peloton Announces Expansion Into Germany, Peloton [Press Release], 22 May, https://www.prnewswire.com/news-releases/peloton-announces-expansion-into-germany-300854763.html (archived at https://perma.cc/CV6C-6R84)

Pietruszynski, G A (nd) Recipe of Viral Features Used by the Fastest-Growing Startups, Neil Patel [Blog], https://neilpatel.com/blog/recipe-of-viral-features/ (archived at https://perma.cc/5GPN-99JJ)

Raeste, J-P (2020) Miljardin Euron Woltti, Helsingin Sanomat, 26 December, https://www.hs.fi/talous/art-2000006657577.html (archived at https://perma.cc/D326-LU5A)

Rinstrom, A and Fares, M (2019) IKEA accelerates services drive as competition stiffens, Reuters, 11 February, https://www.reuters.com/article/us-ikea-services-taskrabbit-focus-idUSKCN1Q00G3 (archived at https://perma.cc/MAF9-4TYR)

Tetra Pak (2020) Tetra Pak launches first virtual marketplace for food and beverage manufacturers, Tetra Pak [Press Release], 22 January, https://www.tetrapak.com/en-gb/about-tetra-pak/news-and-events/newsarchive/virtual-marketplace-food-and-beverage-manufacturers (archived at https://perma.cc/3F3T-GWC7)

Thomas, L (2020) Peloton thinks it can grow to 100 million subscribers. Here's how, CNBC, 15 September, https://www.cnbc.com/2020/09/15/peloton-thinks-it-can-grow-to-100-million-subscribers-heres-how.html (archived at https://perma.cc/VQX3-ZU82)

Varjo (2020) A New Era in Astronaut Training, https://varjo.com/boeing-starliner/ (archived at https://perma.cc/E3JP-BZ6N)

Chapter 4

Baker, J (2018) Uber Eats, Joshua M Baker [Blog], https://www.joshuambaker.com/work-ubereats.html (archived at https://perma.cc/2QEQ-X8AX)

Bergstein B (2020) What AI still can't do, MIT Technology Review, 19 February, https://www.technologyreview.com/2020/02/19/868178/what-ai-still-cant-do/ (archived at https://perma.cc/CNJ7-796K)

Efrati, A (2018) What Makes Tesla's Autopilot Different, The Information, 5 November, https://www.theinformation.com/articles/what-makes-teslas-autopilot-different (archived at https://perma.cc/8RAH-CQRM)

Gill, B (2018) User Stories from the Industry of Things (Part Two), Arc Advisory Group [Blog], 9 August, https://www.arcweb.com/blog/user-stories-industry-things-part-two (archived at https://perma.cc/7BYA-3K2F)

Gleeson, D (2020) Orica leverages MWD data, AI to create new blast loading design benchmark, International Mining, 14 December, https://im-mining.com/2020/12/14/orica-leverages-mwd-data-ai-create-new-blast-loading-design-benchmark/ (archived at https://perma.cc/L2DW-SX4R)

Green, J (2020) Google Cloud AI Platform: Human Data labeling-as-a-Service Part 1, 17 November, https://towardsdatascience.com/google-cloud-ai-platform-human-data-labeling-as-a-service-part-1-170cbe73137b (archived at https://perma.cc/5AY9-ZFZA)

Hawkins, A (2020) Waymo pulls back the curtain on 6.1 million miles of self-driving car data in Phoenix, The Verge, 30 October, https://www.theverge.com/2020/10/30/21538999/waymo-self-driving-car-data-miles-crashes-phoenix-google (archived at https://perma.cc/NJ75-8JY5)

Hermann, J and Del Balso, M (2017) Meet Michelangelo: Uber's Machine Learning Platform, Uber Engineering, 5 September, https://eng.uber.com/michelangelo/ (archived at https://perma.cc/L9AL-5PAX)

Karjaluoto, A and Muranen, K (2020) Industrial data economy for Finland, position paper, Intelligent Industry Ecosystem DIMECC, September, https://www.dimecc.com/wp-content/uploads/2020/09/DIMECC-Industrial-data-economy-for-Finland-PositionPaper-2020-2.pdf (archived at https://perma.cc/UC6H-ED3B)

Lee, T (2019) Tesla just bought an AI startup to improve autopilot—here's what it does, Ars Technica, 10 February, https://arstechnica.com/cars/2019/10/how-teslas-latest-acquisition-could-accelerate-autopilot-development/ (archived at https://perma.cc/74YZ-TZMD)

Martin, N (2019) Uber Charges More If They Think You're Willing To Pay More, Forbes, 30 March, https://www.forbes.com/sites/nicolemartin1/2019/03/30/uber-charges-more-if-they-think-youre-willing-to-pay-more/?sh=5869b8d87365 (archived at https://perma.cc/Y3FL-PVPZ)

Nykänen, A (2019) Healthcare needs explainable human-in-the-loop AI, LinkedIn, 21 May, https://www.linkedin.com/pulse/healthcare-needs-explainable-human-in-the-loop-ai-anna-nyk%C3%A4nen/ (archived at https://perma.cc/WS3J-MYLJ)

O'Kane, S (2018) How Tesla And Waymo Are Tackling A Major Problem For Self-Driving Cars: Data, The Verge, 10 April, https://www.theverge.com/transportation/2018/4/19/17204044/tesla-waymo-self-driving-car-data-simulation (archived at https://perma.cc/VS4N-TBT4)

Ransbotham, S, Khodabandeh, S, Kiron, D, Candelon, F, Chu, M and LaFountain, B (2020) Expanding AI's Impact with Organizational Learning, MIT Sloan Management Review and Boston Consulting Group, October

Schubert, S and Dayan, F H (2020) When is data pooling anticompetitive?, Lexology, 14 December, https://www.lexology.com/library/detail.aspx?g=40bb6970-8419-4f78-90aa-a9e160c61ef7 (archived at https://perma.cc/4BGA-8UYN)

Sherer, L and Cleghorn, J (2018) How Advanced Analytics Is Changing B2B Selling, Harward Business Review, 10 May, hbr.org/2018/05/how-advanced-analytics-is-changing-b2b-selling (archived at https://perma.cc/8SWA-AKH3)

Silo AI (2019a) Finnair and Silo. AI improve situational awareness of air traffic with artificial intelligence, Silo AI [Blog], 23 May, https://silo.ai/finnair-silo-ai-improve-situational-awareness-of-air-traffic/ (archived at https://perma.cc/5SYG-ESUK)

Silo AI (2019b) How artificial intelligence is transforming the water sector: Case Ramboll, Silo AI [Blog], 14 February, https://silo.ai/how-artificial-intelligence-is-transforming-the-water-sector-case-ramboll/ (archived at https://perma.cc/AY69-JJ8Z)

Sinek, S (2020) *The Infinite Game*, Penguin, New York

Technology Industries of Finland (2019) Model terms of the Technology industries for data sharing, Teknova [Webstore], https://teknologiainfo.net/en/content/model-terms-technology-industries-data-sharing (archived at https://perma.cc/7295-7K8W)

Tesla (2019) Tesla Autonomy Day, 22 April, https://www.youtube.com/watch?v=Ucp0TTmvqOE (archived at https://perma.cc/4YAC-8ABV)

Tesla (2020) Future of Driving, https://www.tesla.com/autopilot?redirect=no (archived at https://perma.cc/6KVE-YJ5E)

Uber (2019) Science at Uber: Powering Machine Learning at Uber, 9 September, https://www.youtube.com/watch?v=DOwDIHzN5bs (archived at https://perma.cc/E5RB-ZUFC)

Wang, Z (2019) Predicting Time to Cook, Arrive, and Deliver at Uber Eats, InfoQ, 20 November, https://www.infoq.com/articles/uber-eats-time-predictions/ (archived at https://perma.cc/LL4N-JBF9)

Chapter 5

Adobe (2019) The Platform Economy: Why APIs And Integrations Are Crucial, Adobe [Blog], 12 May, https://blog.adobe.com/en/publish/2019/05/12/entering-the-platform-economy-why-apis-and-integrations-are-crucial.html#gs.r3ll0z (archived at https://perma.cc/YU76-UC2M)

Akana (2014) John Deere is Using APIs to Grow the World's Food Supply, Akana [Blog], 18 November, https://www.akana.com/blog/john-deere-using-apis-grow-worlds-food-supply (archived at https://perma.cc/DJ2E-BJU7)

Boyd, M (2017) Five Metrics Every API Strategy Should Measure, Hitch [Blog], 18 January, https://blog.hitchhq.com/five-metrics-every-api-strategy-should-measure-691596075b6 (archived at https://perma.cc/42R6-LMSQ)

Dellinger, A J (2013) #FirstWorldProblems: Twitter third party clients continue to shut down, and its API is just getting more restrictive, digitaltrends, 18 March, https://www.digitaltrends.com/mobile/firstworldproblems-twitter-api-and-third-party-problem/ (archived at https://perma.cc/3F9D-L8QV)

Endler, M (2017) How API Management Accelerates Digital Business, apigee [Blog], 18 September, https://medium.com/apis-and-digital-transformation/how-api-management-accelerates-digital-business-4ccea9b302df (archived at https://perma.cc/G6M7-N3WD)

Glas, G (2020) What is an API and SDK? app press, https://www.app-press.com/blog/what-is-an-api-and-sdk (archived at https://perma.cc/DJW9-8FG8)

Glickenhouse, A (2017) Building APIs for the Manufacturing Industry, IBM [blog], 30 June, https://developer.ibm.com/apiconnect/2017/06/30/building-apis-manufacturing-industry/ (archived at https://perma.cc/DSU3-F9HL)

Iyengar, K, Khanna, S, Ramadath, S and Stephens, D (2017) What it really takes to capture the value of APIs, McKinsey Digital, 12 September, https://www.mckinsey.com/business-functions/mckinsey-digital/our-insights/what-it-really-takes-to-capture-the-value-of-apis (archived at https://perma.cc/UB55-FN6Z)

John Deere (2020) 7th Annual Develop with Deere Conference Focuses on Digital Connectivity, John Deere [Press Release], 4 February, https://www.deere.com/en/our-company/news-and-announcements/news-releases/2020/agriculture/2020feb04-develop-with-deere-conference/ (archived at https://perma.cc/XQ89-TJDT)

KONE (2019) An ecosystem of opportunities, KONE [Blog], 29 November, https://www.kone.com/en/news-and-insights/stories/an-ecosystem-of-opportunities.aspx (archived at https://perma.cc/DSP7-WGH7)

Kramer, S D (2011) The biggest thing Amazon got right: The Platform, GigaOm [Blog], 10 October, https://gigaom.com/2011/10/12/419-the-biggest-thing-amazon-got-right-the-platform/ (archived at https://perma.cc/TQ5Q-8R3R)

Levine, D (2019) APIs are the next big SaaS wave, Techcrunch [Blog], 6 September, https://techcrunch.com/2019/09/06/apis-are-the-next-big-saas-wave/ (archived at https://perma.cc/V8DP-STAJ)

Manning, L (2020) Leaf Agriculture comes out of stealth with agtech API to integrate your farm data, AFN, 11 February, https://agfundernews.com/leaf-agriculture-comes-out-of-stealth-with-agtech-api-to-integrate-your-farm-data.html (archived at https://perma.cc/EXZ5-RS4R)

Mersch, V (2016) Twitter's 10 Year Struggle with Developer Relations, Nordic API [Blog], 23 March, https://nordicapis.com/twitter-10-year-struggle-with-developer-relations/ (archived at https://perma.cc/K9QP-ZNZV)

ProgrammableWeb (2021) API Directory, ProgrammableWeb [Company website], https://www.programmableweb.com/apis/directory (archived at https://perma.cc/953U-R5UG)

Salmikuukka (2020) personal interview

Skyscanner (2021) Travel APIs, Skyscanner [Company website], https://www.partners.skyscanner.net/affiliates/travel-apis (archived at https://perma.cc/X6M8-F4QL)

SuccessfulFarming (2020) How develop with Deere 2020 connects the dots, SuccessfulFarming [Video], 13 February, https://www.agriculture.com/video/how-develop-with-deere-2020-connects-the-dots (archived at https://perma.cc/4AJU-FJXN)

Williams, J (2020) What is a developer program and what does it take to build one? [Blog], 18 March, https://www.jesse-williams.com/what-is-a-developer-program (archived at https://perma.cc/B94S-J5N6)

Wintrob, G (2017) How the Flexport API enables global trade, GET PUT POST [Blog], 22 February, https://getputpost.co/how-the-flexport-api-enables-global-trade-92b9131d4bd4 (archived at https://perma.cc/QE3E-HJGB)

Chapter 6

Barney J (1991) Firm Resources and Sustained Competitive Advantage, *Journal of Management*, **17** (1): pp 99–120

Barsade, S G (2002) The Ripple Effect: Emotional Contagion and its Influence on Group Behavior, *Administrative Science Quarterly*, **47** (4), pp 644–75

Bohn, D (2019) Amazon says 100 million Alexa devices have been sold – what's next?, The Verge, 4 January, https://www.theverge.com/2019/1/4/18168565/amazon-alexa-devices-how-many-sold-number-100-million-dave-limp (archived at https://perma.cc/LP47-XE6F)

Business Insider (2017) 7 potential bidders, a call to Amazon, and an ultimatum: How the Whole Foods deal went down, Business Insider, 29 December, https://www.businessinsider.com/breaking-it-down-amazon-tough-negotiations-how-the-whole-foods-deal-went-down-2017-12?r=US&IR=T (archived at https://perma.cc/PTL6-HPL8)

Campbell, T (2018) Should Amazon's PillPack Acquisition Frighten Pharmacies?, The Motley Fool, 28 June, https://www.fool.com/investing/2018/06/28/should-amazons-pillpocket-acquisition-frighten-pha.aspx (archived at https://perma.cc/WF4D-Z9QF)

Cheddar (2019) Facebook Makes First Blockchain Acquisition With Chainspace: Sources, https://cheddar.com/media/facebook-blockchain-acquisition-chainspace (archived at https://perma.cc/D5RD-AJZ6)

Edmondson A (2019) *The Fearless Organization*, Wiley, New York

Farr, C (2019) The inside story of why Amazon bought PillPack in its effort to crack the $500 billion prescription market, CNBC, 10 May, https://www.cnbc.com/2019/05/10/why-amazon-bought-pillpack-for-753-million-and-what-happens-next.html (archived at https://perma.cc/3Q35-AU93)

Fredrickson, B L (2001) The role of positive emotions in positive psychology: The broaden-and-build theory of positive emotions, *American Psychologist*, **56** (3), pp 218–26

Gavetti, G, Levinthal, D A and Rivkin, J W (2005) Strategy Making in Novel and Complex Worlds: The Power of Analogy, *Strategic Management Journal*, **26** (8), pp 691–712

GSM Arena (2019) Flashback: the Motorola ROKR E1 was a dud, but it paved the way for the iPhone, https://www.gsmarena.com/flashback_the_motorola_rokr_e1_was_a_dud_but_it_paved_the_way_for_the_iphone-news-38934.php (archived at https://perma.cc/WTP8-WPXS)

Gurman, M and Bloomberg (2021) Apple's self-driving electric car is at least half a decade away, Fortune, 7 January, https://fortune.com/2021/01/07/apples-self-driving-electric-car-half-a-decade-away/ (archived at https://perma.cc/JW2J-8GGU)

Healey, M P, Vuori, T O. and Hodgkinson, G P (2015) When teams agree while disagreeing: Reflexion and reflection in shared cognition, *Academy of Management Review*, **40** (3), pp 399-422

Hunter, P G and Schellenberg, E G (2010) Music and Emotion, in *Music Perception*, ed M Riess Jones, R Fay and A Popper, Springer Handbook of Auditory Research, vol 36, Springer, New York, NY, https://doi.org/10.1007/978-1-4419-6114-3_5 (archived at https://perma.cc/5W86-2WDV)

Isaac, M (2019) Zuckerberg Plans to Integrate WhatsApp, Instagram and Facebook Messenger, *The New York Times*, 15 January, https://www.nytimes.com/2019/01/25/technology/facebook-instagram-whatsapp-messenger.html (archived at https://perma.cc/7KFD-M82T)

Korosec, K (2019) Elon Musk predicts Tesla energy could be 'bigger' than its EV business, Techcrunch, 24 October, https://techcrunch.com/2019/10/23/elon-musk-predicts-tesla-energy-could-be-bigger-than-its-ev-business/ (archived at https://perma.cc/X6JS-3N56)

Lunden, I (2018) WhatsApp will not share user data with Facebook until it complies with GDPR, ICO closes investigation, Techcrunch, 14 March, https://techcrunch.com/2018/03/14/whatsapp-will-not-share-user-data-with-facebook-until-it-complies-with-gdpr-ico-closes-investigation/ (archived at https://perma.cc/9ARJ-9AYA)

MacRumors (2021) Apple Car – Apple's vehicle project, focused on building an autonomous driving car, MacRumors, 19 January, https://www.macrumors.com/roundup/apple-car/ (archived at https://perma.cc/L88G-4NSU)

Meeker (2016) Internet Trends 2016, Kleiner Perkins, 1 June, https://www.kleinerperkins.com/perspectives/2016-internet-trends-report/ (archived at https://perma.cc/87QG-6465)

Miller, R (2016), How AWS came to be, Techcruch, 2 July, https://techcrunch.com/2016/07/02/andy-jassys-brief-history-of-the-genesis-of-aws/ (archived at https://perma.cc/2DLM-EUZS)

Miller, R (2019) Plaid puts Quovo acquisition right to work with new investments product, Techcrunch, 20 June, https://techcrunch.com/2019/06/20/plaid-puts-quovo-acquisition-right-to-work-with-new-investments-product/ (archived at https://perma.cc/6YX9-HT8A)

Phelps, E A, Lempert, K A and Sokol-Hessner, P (2014) Emotion and Decision Making: Multiple Modulatory Neural Circuits, *Annual Review of Neuroscience*, 37 (1), pp 263–87

Praszkier, R (2016) Empathy, mirror neurons and SYNC, *Mind & Society*, 15 (1), pp 1–25

Soper, S and Giammona, C (2017) Amazon Said to Mull Whole Foods Bid Before Jana Stepped In, Bloomberg, 12 April, https://www.bloomberg.com/news/articles/2017-04-11/amazon-said-to-mull-bid-for-whole-foods-before-jana-stepped-in (archived at https://perma.cc/87WN-J62K)

Target (2017) Here's How Acquiring Shipt Will Bring Same-Day Delivery to About Half of Target Stores in Early 2018, A Bullseye View, 13 December, https://corporate.target.com/article/2017/12/target-acquires-shipt (archived at https://perma.cc/CK32-7LMD)

Target (2020a) A Closer Look at Target's Q3 2020, A Bullseye View, 18 November, https://corporate.target.com/article/2020/11/q3-2020-earnings (archived at https://perma.cc/R66H-T68R)

Target (2020b) Target Corporation Reports Third Quarter Earnings, A Bullseye View, 18 November, https://corporate.target.com/press/releases/2020/11/Target-Corporation-Reports-Third-Quarter-Earnings (archived at https://perma.cc/4L35-F7Y2)

Chapter 7

aito.ai (2018) Boosting Knowledge Management: How agile AI experiments can help big companies like Futurice identify who knows what within their organisation, https://aitodotai.medium.com/boosting-knowledge-management-how-agile-ai-experiments-can-help-big-companies-like-futurice-daad96e49705 (archived at https://perma.cc/X5QD-9Y37)

Asikainen, A (2020) *Aiding Software Project Staffing by Utilizing Recommendation Systems*, Master's thesis, Aalto University, Finland, https://aaltodoc.aalto.fi/

bitstream/handle/123456789/46107/master_Asikainen_Aleksi_2020.
pdf?sequence=1&isAllowed=y (archived at https://perma.cc/2PH4-UN2C)

Boston Dynamics (2020) Spot improves construction site documentation for
Pomerleau, https://www.bostondynamics.com/spot/applications/pomerleau
(archived at https://perma.cc/CXQ3-3P6Z)

DARPA (2021) Explainable Artificial Intelligence (XAI), https://www.darpa.mil/
program/explainable-artificial-intelligence (archived at https://perma.cc/326C-S6UE)

Duhigg, C (2016) What Google Learned From Its Quest to Build the Perfect Team,
The New York Times Magazine, 25 February, https://www.nytimes.com/2016/02/28/
magazine/what-google-learned-from-its-quest-to-build-the-perfect-team.
html?smid=pl-share (archived at https://perma.cc/EFJ5-DXQF)

IBM (2018) Building a winning team using AI, IBM Research [Blog], 16 March,
https://www.ibm.com/blogs/research/2018/03/build-winning-teams-using-ai/
(archived at https://perma.cc/68YB-D84X)

IBM (2021) Explainable AI, https://www.ibm.com/watson/explainable-ai (archived at
https://perma.cc/8RJ5-2BGG)

Murray A, Rhymer, J and Sirmon, D G (2021) Humans and Technology: Forms of
Conjoined Agency in Organizations, *Academy of Management Review*, in press,
https://journals.aom.org/doi/abs/10.5465/amr.2019.0186 (archived at
https://perma.cc/D9N3-RE4B)

Peng, N Y (2020) How Renaissance beat the markets with Machine Learning, Towards
Data Science, 3 January, https://towardsdatascience.com/how-renaissance-beat-the-
markets-with-machine-learning-606b17577797 (archived at https://perma.cc/
V93L-JFT8)

Ransbotham, S, Khodabandeh, S, Kiron, D, Candelon, F, Chu, M and LaFountain, B
(2020) Expanding AI's Impact With Organizational Learning, MIT Sloan
Management Review and Boston Consulting Group, October

re:Work (nd) Guide: Understand team effectiveness, https://rework.withgoogle.com/
print/guides/5721312655835136/ (archived at https://perma.cc/JJ7F-YMN9)

Sensoneo (2021) [Company website], https://sensoneo.com (archived at https://perma.cc/
Y3L4-A2UU)

Stenius, H and Vuori, T O. (2018) Change Analytics: How Data-Analytics Can
Improve Top-Down Change Communication, *Academy of Management Proceedings*,
1, https://journals.aom.org/doi/10.5465/AMBPP.2018.12326abstract (archived at
https://perma.cc/T3MM-G7XY)

Trimble (2019) Trimble, Hilti and Boston Dynamics Partner to Explore the Use of
Autonomous Robots in Construction [News Release], 19 November,
https://www.trimble.com/news/release.aspx?id=111919a (archived at
https://perma.cc/X2UU-XDDR)

Tyre, M J and Orlikowski, W J (1994) Windows of opportunity: Temporal patterns of
technological adaptation in organizations, *Organization Science*, 5 (1), pp 98–113

Zoan (nd) Situational Awareness – Client: Finnair, https://zoan.fi/work/finnair-situational-awareness/ (archived at https://perma.cc/DDR5-64B4)

Conclusions

Butcher, S (2020) The real reason Marco Argenti joined Goldman Sachs from AWS, efinancialcareers, 31 January, https://www.efinancialcareers.com/news/2020/01/marco-argenti-goldman-sachs (archived at https://perma.cc/S7KR-7DQ7)

Campbell and DeFrancesco (2019) Goldman Sachs' new CTO shares his strategy for attracting outside developers to work more closely with the bank, giving a glimpse into the future of how Wall Street will work, Insider, 7 November, https://www.businessinsider.com/goldman-sachs-incoming-cto-atte-lahtiranta-interview-2019-11?r=US&IR=T (archived at https://perma.cc/7BRM-GCA8)

Crosman, P (2021) How new robo adviser fits into Goldman's tech strategy, American Banker, 18 February, https://www.americanbanker.com/news/how-goldmans-new-robo-adviser-fits-into-its-tech-strategy (archived at https://perma.cc/ZEZ2-F5W6)

Gates, B (2021) *How to Avoid a Climate Disaster: The Solutions We Have and the Breakthroughs We Need*, Diversified Publishing, Murfreesboro, TN

Kotorchevikj, I (2020) Why and how Nokia changed the game with people analytics, Hyperight [Webinar], 25 August, https://read.hyperight.com/why-and-how-nokia-changed-the-game-with-people-analytics/ (archived at https://perma.cc/47A2-YKCD)

O'Halloran, J (2020), Nokia launches AI-based operations to help telcos enter the 5G era, Computer Weekly, 31 March, https://www.computerweekly.com/news/252480922/Nokia-launches-AI-based-operations-to-help-telcos-enter-the-5G-era (archived at https://perma.cc/6TL5-GZNE)

Olson, P (2017) Nokia Buys Comptel For $370 Million To Help It Woo Telcos, Forbes, 9 February, https://www.forbes.com/sites/parmyolson/2017/02/09/nokia-buys-comptel-for-370-million-to-help-it-woo-telcos/?sh=685addb81939 (archived at https://perma.cc/9JV4-2WEC)

Rodgers, L (2018) Climate change: The massive CO2 emitter you may not know about, BBC News, 17 December, https://www.bbc.com/news/science-environment-46455844 (archived at https://perma.cc/7RLN-J2BL)

Siilasmaa, R (2018) The Chairman of Nokia on Ensuring Every Employee Has a Basic Understanding of Machine Learning – Including Him, Harvard Business Review [Blog], 4 October, hbr.org/2018/10/the-chairman-of-nokia-on-ensuring-every-employee-has-a-basic-understanding-of-machine-learning-including-him (archived at https://perma.cc/7K2W-PJ4Z)

Vuori, T O. and Huy, N (2018) How Nokia Embraced the Emotional Side of Strategy, Harvard Business Review (digital article), hbr.org/2018/05/how-nokia-embraced-the-emotional-side-of-strategy (archived at https://perma.cc/XD36-Q56M)

Vuori, T O. and Huy, N (2021) Regulating Top Managers' Emotions during Strategy Making, Nokia's Distributed Approach Enabling Radical Change from Mobile Phones to Networks in 2007–2013, *Academy of Management Journal*, in press, https://journals.aom.org/doi/10.5465/amj.2019.0865?ai=vctv&ui=3os1&af=H (archived at https://perma.cc/W8WF-5MUU)

X (2021) The Everyday Robot Project, X – The Moonshot Factory, https://x.company/ projects/everyday-robots/ (archived at https://perma.cc/BJ4E-T5RE)

Index